The Hungry Ear

The Hungry Ear

POEMS OF FOOD & DRINK

Kevin Young

BLOOMSBURY

NEW YORK · LONDON · NEW DELHI · SYDNEY

Published by Bloomsbury USA, New York

All papers used by Bloomsbury USA are natural, recyclable products made
from wood grown in well-managed forests. The manufacturing processes
conform to the environmental regulations of the country of origin.

LIBRARY OF CONGRESS CATALOGING-IN-PUBLICATION DATA HAS BEEN APPLIED FOR.

ISBN: 978-1-60819-551-0

First U.S. Edition 2012

3   5   7   9   10   8   6   4   2

Text design by Sara Stemen
Printed in the U.S.A.

for my mother

who taught me how

to cook & to listen

Wine is bottled poetry.
—ROBERT LOUIS STEVENSON

*On our earth, before writing was invented, before the printing
press was invented, poetry flourished. That is why we know poetry
is like bread; it should be shared by all, by scholars and by peasants,
by all our vast, incredible, extraordinary family of humanity.*
—PABLO NERUDA

Hunger is the best sauce.
—CHEF SAYING

CONTENTS

II. Wintering 73

III. Spring Rain

IV. Sweet Summer

INTRODUCTION

Love, satisfaction, trouble, death, pleasure, work, sex, memory, celebration, hunger, desire, loss, laughter, even salvation: to all these things food can provide a prelude; or comfort after; and sometimes a handy substitute for. It often seems food is a metaphor for most anything, from justice to joy. Perhaps too easy of a metaphor—sometimes food is just food. Still, there is nothing like food and drink to remind us of life's pleasures, sating far more than hunger.

A good meal provides such sustenance not just out of need, but out of a whole host of things, whether reminding us of our childhoods, or grandparents, or the old country—or teaching us about a new one. Food transports us to another place like little else, even if it's just the couch after Thanksgiving turkey. I have put together this anthology to honor food's unique yet multifaceted pleasures. Nothing is as necessary yet as taken for granted these days as food—except maybe poetry. Both are bread and honey, water and wine, mother's milk and manna; and if ignored, or never used, both wither. Poetry keeps body and soul together and remarks upon what makes the human animal both one with and apart from the world.

Perhaps this is why I have never met a group more reliable to have a good meal with—and it should be said, a few drinks with—than poets. (Southerners are a close second.) Whether that meal means hunks of cheese sliced off with a knife alongside crusty bread and cheap wine; or enough homemade stew to feed a fort (or loft, or shared house); an extravagant feast on someone else's dime; or a nip of an uncle's moonshine: poets sure do throw down around the table. This, I think, is not just because a poet's next meal may always be in doubt, but because poets tend to love the details, the process of food,

1

the languid hours of a good meal—meaning not just the vittles but the talk, often loud, that accompanies it.

This may also be because the best poems, like the best meals, are made from scratch. Both rely on the seasons, but also human history; both also consist of tradition, on knowledge passed down either from books or from generation to generation, hand to mouth. In poetry, there are few shortcuts, but there are secrets. Food and poetry each insist the we put our own twists and ingredients in the mix: we make each dish, like a good poem, our own. With any luck, the result is both surprising and satisfying, exactly what we wanted, perhaps without even knowing it.

However, we know too well the ways in which our society has abandoned good food, and too often poetry entirely—as if it grows without our water and light, and that our neglect won't reveal itself. "Can one be inspired by rows of prepared canned meals?" asks Alice B. Toklas, who knew her way around both poetry and a kitchen, publishing her famous cookbook after her life partner, Gertrude Stein, passed away. "Never. One must get nearer to creation to be able to create, even in the kitchen."

Luckily, there seems to be a surge in returning to real food—some would say "slow food," as opposed to fast—and if there's hope for what we insist we and our children eat, this may mean a world where poetry too can return to the table, where not just conversation, but culture, is made.

A seat at / the common table: this dream, shared by poet and pauper alike, is found in these pages.

In one crucial way, food differs from writing: food is temporary. It is exactly this fact, as many a writer will tell you, wherein the sublime pleasure of cooking really lies. After a long day of trying to be immortal, or at least get to the end of the blank page or screen— rather symbolically hitting SAVE—there is something satisfying in getting your hands dirty, in making something that has, necessarily, an obvious end point. With food, the better it is, the less it sticks around.

(Except the way good food "sticks to your ribs" in the parlance of where I come from.) Temporariness is one of food's best qualities, making it something other than the chore that good writing can be. This is the opposite of good reading, in which the better it is the faster it flies. It is these fleeting yet everlasting pleasures that this anthology explores.

Moving through the seasons, from First Harvest to Sweet Summer, the cycle of life is shown here in its ups and downs—as only poetry can. Like the rallying cry of recent food advocates, my motto in picking these poems has been "Eat Local"—and like I say to my son, "Eat what you like"—I have been driven to include poets who write of the world around us and whose work makes my mouth water. What follows is a feast for the eyes and ear, one ranging from Pablo Neruda's famous odes to William Matthews's "Onions" to a host of evocations of blackberry picking—from Mary Oliver to Seamus Heaney; Galway Kinnell to Robert Hass to Yusef Komunyakaa. Indeed, there turn out to be a lot of fine blackberry poems, perhaps because they are both plentiful and primal. As a result, the anthology starts there, and like the seasons, circles back there, too. Along the way, we hear from James Beard Award–winning chefs like Linton Hopkins and, even in epigraphs, Julia Child and other homegrown cooks like Toklas; we sing along with drinking songs from Yeats and poems turned pop songs by Wyn Cooper, while enduring hangovers with James Wright. We visit questions of custom, memory, economy (in both the financial and poetic senses), and desire. We taste the bitterness of death, as well as the soothing food after.

I have written elsewhere—in my previous anthology, *The Art of Losing*, and in my own food odes—of the healing power of food after loss. It is a tradition I know best from the African-American repast, but it can easily be seen in many others: from the Midwestern casserole or Southern collard greens brought to the house of mourning to an Irish wake, toasting those gone. Such meals and drink, whether sweet tea or hard cider, remind us we're alive, while also making us realize: what else can we do but provide some sustenance for those whose only meal otherwise may be sorrow?

Food also helps us to celebrate, to mark an occasion as well as a season—from birthday cake to egg nog; from "praise wine" to the bread of high holy days. The result, seen here, is the presence of food as both an everyday and extraordinary festivity—which is where, alongside poetry, it belongs.

Sad to say, Thanksgiving remains the only homemade meal many Americans still have. Whether in soup kitchens or in their family's gathering place, such a meal represents not only fuel, but a form of welcome. Just like giving a helping hand, giving thanks is one thing we should try to do more than once a year. If we did, perhaps we would find ourselves more connected to the earth and ocean and each other, something I think that food—breaking bread, as it were—can do.

No wonder that when African Americans sought their too-often-denied rights as full-fledged Americans during the civil rights movement they chose the lunch counter to wage their struggle. Freedom or its lack particularly smarts when it involves food, or clean water, or one's own culture—things we all need and too often are denied. The gall of such denial angered my father, once forced to carry his lunch in a brown bag in the segregated South—just as he had to make sure he didn't have to go to the restroom when out in that separate, unequal world. Later in life, he declared he never would carry a lunch bag, or its indignity.

Food, like poetry, after all, is a necessity, a human need—and so food also signals justice, and its triumph. Once my mother and I ate at a restaurant in Baton Rouge, a nice lunch eatery that served meals cafeteria style. While we were in line, she remarked, almost off-handedly, that she and her friends down the road at all-black Southern University had made a pilgrimage there years earlier to help desegregate the restaurant we were standing in. Such a journey hadn't stopped with her visit twenty years before, but continued even on that day; it was a different kind of cycle that meal marked. Her telling me let me know, however indirectly, not just about sacrifice, but the dailiness of it. And that sometimes, the welcome table is something we must insist upon ourselves. *I, too, sing America.*

Food too can be where we experience, or even reclaim, culture. Not only is it where we declare our values—or what we like—but also some of what we aspire to. In the words of Chef Julia Child, "How can a nation be great if its bread tastes like Kleenex?"

We, too, wish to grow. Food can not only be a way, say, of celebrating red beans and rice, or rice and black beans, or fried rice, or basmati, or long grain, or any version of rice that you can imagine—but it can provide our first experience of another world of taste and temperature. The table is literally where we experience the spice of life; and learn the names of spices in other tongues. Food is often our first adventure with another culture and a way we learn to measure our own.

Or do I mean poetry is? This anthology revels in the many tastes all around us, some of which we need poetry to help describe.

The ritual of cooking and eating, in the course of human history, has traditionally involved not just what we could grow from the earth, but what we could tend, milk, feed, gather, fish, hunt, or slaughter. I don't mean to put such need above others—we should eat a balanced meal—but it is easy to judge the eating of others, and easy to feel self-righteous about food. And yet what gets lost in the litany of diets and healthier-than-thou discussions is the food itself. The pleasure of a plum, fresh from the icebox, *so delicious / and so cold.* Or the taste of fresh milk, or real butter, or the sounds even of the cows on my grandparents' farm—food is not just fuel, but an experience, and one we'd do well to honor the full range of.

You'll see vegetables here—be sure to eat those, please—and plenty fruit, but you'll also find "Beer for Breakfast" and bacon for dessert. Here is the full range of eating, from pork—about which there seem enough poems to warrant its own section—to peaches, from "the meat of memory" to the need for forgetting. This book's menu is as omnivorous as my poetic taste. I have sought, like the poets here, to

*

5

sometimes consider the difficulties of the dilemma of killing things to live. The sacrifice involved in preparing food not merely economic, but at times gendered, as Mary Oliver reminds us in her poem about life on a farm. We also consider the lobster—one of the only foods remaining often brought home live by those who eat it, which, if some see as cruel, at least is honest. "The pleasure of eating should be an extensive pleasure, not that of the mere gourmet," poet and farmer Wendell Berry writes. He could be speaking of poetry too. Berry reminds us that "the knowledge of the good health of the garden relieves and frees and comforts the eater. The same goes for eating meat. The thought of the good pasture and of the calf contentedly grazing flavors the steak. Some, I know, will think it bloodthirsty or worse to eat a fellow creature you have known all its life. On the contrary, I think it means that you eat with understanding and with gratitude." As the farmer knows, like my grandparents who raised livestock and connected to the source, food is not mere fuel or fetish, but, ultimately, praise.

Such everyday praise—of coffee and collards, of appetite and loss, salt and honey and hot peppers and "American Milk," of the human body and the greening world—is this anthology's aim. The poems often focus on what we might call "source foods," foods in their natural, whole, and ingredient states. We too seek the source: may finding it, alongside the poets here, leave you sated, yet wanting more tomorrow. Please join me at the table.

In the words of my grandmother, *Help yourself.*

—KEVIN YOUNG
Decatur, Georgia

Perhaps the World Ends Here

JOY HARJO

The world begins at a kitchen table. No matter what, we must eat
to live.

The gifts of earth are brought and prepared, set on the table. So it has
been since creation, and it will go on.

We chase chickens or dogs away from it. Babies teethe at the corners.
They scrape their knees under it.

It is here that children are given instructions on what it means to be
human. We make men at it, we make women.

At this table we gossip, recall enemies and the ghosts of lovers.

Our dreams drink coffee with us as they put their arms around our
children. They laugh with us at our poor falling-down selves
and as we put ourselves back together once again at the table.

This table has been a house in the rain, an umbrella in the sun.

Wars have begun and ended at this table. It is a place to hide in the
shadow of terror. A place to celebrate the terrible victory.

We have given birth on this table, and have prepared our parents for
burial here.

At this table we sing with joy, with sorrow. We pray of suffering and remorse. We give thanks.

Perhaps the world will end at the kitchen table, while we are laughing and crying, eating of the last sweet bite.

I.
Harvest Moon

I praise the fall: it is the human season.
—ARCHIBALD MACLEISH

FIRST HARVEST

I begin with the proposition that eating is an agricultural act.
—WENDELL BERRY
"THE PLEASURES OF EATING"

August

MARY OLIVER

When the blackberries hang
swollen in the woods, in the brambles
nobody owns, I spend

all day among the high
branches, reaching
my ripped arms, thinking

of nothing, cramming
the black honey of summer
into my mouth; all day my body

accepts what it is. In the dark
creeks that run by there is
this thick paw of my life darting among

the black bells, the leaves; there is
this happy tongue.

Blackberry-Picking

SEAMUS HEANEY

Late August, given heavy rain and sun
For a full week, the blackberries would ripen
At first, just one, a glossy purple clot
Among others, red, green, hard as a knot.
You ate that first one and its flesh was sweet
Like thickened wine: summer's blood was in it
Leaving stains upon the tongue and lust for
Picking. Then red ones inked up and that hunger

Sent us out with milk-cans, pea-tins, jam-pots
Where briars scratched and wet grass bleached our boots.
Round hayfields, cornfields and potato drills
We trekked and picked until the cans were full,
Until the tinkling bottom had been covered
With green ones, and on top big dark blobs burned
Like a plate of eyes. Our hands were peppered
With thorn pricks, our palms sticky as Bluebeard's.

We hoarded the fresh berries in the byre.
But when the bath was filled we found a fur,
A rat-grey fungus, glutting on our cache.
The juice was stinking too. Once off the bush
The fruit fermented, the sweet flesh would turn sour.
I always felt like crying. It wasn't fair
That all the lovely canfuls smelt of rot.
Each year I hoped they'd keep, knew they would not.

Meditation at Lagunitas

ROBERT HASS

All the new thinking is about loss.
In this it resembles all the old thinking.
The idea, for example, that each particular erases
the luminous clarity of a general idea. That the clown-
faced woodpecker probing the dead sculpted trunk
of that black birch is, by his presence,
some tragic falling off from a first world
of undivided light. Or the other notion that,
because there is in this world no one thing
to which the bramble of *blackberry* corresponds,
a word is elegy to what it signifies.
We talked about it late last night and in the voice
of my friend, there was a thin wire of grief, a tone
almost querulous. After a while I understood that,
talking this way, everything dissolves: *justice,
pine, hair, woman, you* and *I.* There was a woman
I made love to and I remembered how, holding
her small shoulders in my hands sometimes,
I felt a violent wonder at her presence
like a thirst for salt, for my childhood river
with its island willows, silly music from the pleasure boat,
muddy places where we caught the little orange-silver fish
called *pumpkinseed.* It hardly had to do with her.
Longing, we say, because desire is full
of endless distances. I must have been the same to her.
But I remember so much, the way her hands dismantled bread,
the thing her father said that hurt her, what

she dreamed. There are moments when the body is as numinous
as words, days that are the good flesh continuing.
Such tenderness, those afternoons and evenings,
saying *blackberry, blackberry, blackberry.*

Blackberry Eating

GALWAY KINNELL

I love to go out in late September
among the fat, overripe, icy, black blackberries
to eat blackberries for breakfast,
the stalks very prickly, a penalty
they earn for knowing the black art
of blackberry making; and as I stand among them
lifting the stalks to my mouth, the ripest berries
fall almost unbidden to my tongue,
as words sometimes do, certain peculiar words
like *strengths* or *squinched* or *broughamed*,
many-lettered, one-syllabled lumps,
which I squeeze, squinch open, and splurge well
in the silent, startled, icy, black language
of blackberry eating in late September.

Blackberries

YUSEF KOMUNYAKAA

They left my hands like a printer's
Or thief's before a police blotter
& pulled me into early morning's
Terrestrial sweetness, so thick
The damp ground was consecrated
Where they fell among a garland of thorns.

Although I could smell old lime-covered
History, at ten I'd still hold out my hands
& berries fell into them. Eating from one
& filling a half gallon with the other,
I ate the mythology & dreamt
Of pies and cobbler, almost

Needful as forgiveness. My bird dog Spot
Eyed blue jays & thrashers. The mud frogs
In rich blackness, hid from daylight.
An hour later, beside City Limits Road
I balanced a gleaming can in each hand,
Limboed between worlds, repeating one dollar.

The big blue car made me sweat.
Wintertime crawled out of the windows.
When I leaned closer I saw the boy
& girl my age, in the wide back seat
Smirking, & it was then I remembered my fingers
Burning with thorns among berries too ripe to touch.

Fall

WENDELL BERRY

The wild cherries ripen, black and fat,
Paradisal fruits that taste of no man's sweat.

Reach up, pull down the laden branch, and eat;
When you have learned their bitterness, they taste sweet.

Vespers

LOUISE GLÜCK

In your extended absence, you permit me
use of earth, anticipating
some return on investment. I must report
failure in my assignment, principally
regarding the tomato plants.
I think I should not be encouraged to grow
tomatoes. Or, if I am, you should withhold
the heavy rains, the cold nights that come
so often here, while other regions get
twelve weeks of summer. All this
belongs to you: on the other hand,
I planted the seeds, I watched the first shoots
like wings tearing the soil, and it was my heart
broken by the blight, the black spot so quickly
multiplying in the rows. I doubt
you have a heart, in our understanding of
that term. You who do not discriminate
between the dead and the living, who are, in consequence,
immune to foreshadowing, you may not know
how much terror we bear, the spotted leaf,
the red leaves of the maple falling
even in August, in early darkness: I am responsible
for these vines.

Pokeberries

RUTH STONE

I started out in the Virginia mountains
with my grandma's pansy bed
and my Aunt Maud's dandelion wine.
We lived on greens and back-fat and biscuits.
My Aunt Maud scrubbed right through the linoleum.
My daddy was a Northerner who played drums
and chewed tobacco and gambled.
He married my mama on the rebound.
Who would want an ignorant hill girl with red hair?
They took a Pullman up to Indianapolis
and someone stole my daddy's wallet.
My whole life has been stained with pokeberries.
No man seemed right for me. I was awkward
until I found a good wood-burning stove.
There is no use asking what it means.
With my first piece of ready cash I bought my own
place in Vermont; kerosene lamps, dirt road.
I'm sticking here like a porcupine up a tree.
Like the one our neighbor shot. Its bones and skin
hung there for three years in the orchard.
No amount of knowledge can shake my grandma out of me;
or my Aunt Maud; or my mama, who didn't just bite an apple
with her big white teeth. She split it in two.

After Apple-Picking

ROBERT FROST

My long two-pointed ladder's sticking through a tree
Toward heaven still,
And there's a barrel that I didn't fill
Beside it, and there may be two or three
Apples I didn't pick upon some bough.
But I am done with apple-picking now.
Essence of winter sleep is on the night,
The scent of apples: I am drowsing off.
I cannot rub the strangeness from my sight
I got from looking through a pane of glass
I skimmed this morning from the drinking trough
And held against the world of hoary grass.
It melted, and I let it fall and break.
But I was well
Upon my way to sleep before it fell,
And I could tell
What form my dreaming was about to take.
Magnified apples appear and disappear,
Stem end and blossom end,
And every fleck of russet showing clear.
My instep arch not only keeps the ache,
It keeps the pressure of a ladder-round.
I feel the ladder sway as the boughs bend.
And I keep hearing from the cellar bin
The rumbling sound
Of load on load of apples coming in.
For I have had too much

Of apple-picking: I am overtired
Of the great harvest I myself desired.
There were ten thousand thousand fruit to touch,
Cherish in hand, lift down, and not let fall.
For all
That struck the earth,
No matter if not bruised or spiked with stubble,
Went surely to the cider-apple heap
As of no worth.
One can see what will trouble
This sleep of mine, whatever sleep it is.
Were he not gone,
The woodchuck could say whether it's like his
Long sleep, as I describe its coming on,
Or just some human sleep.

A Short History of the Apple

DORIANNE LAUX

The crunch is the thing, a certain joy in crashing
through living tissue, a memory of Neanderthal days.
—EDWARD BUNYAN, *The Anatomy of Dessert*, 1929

Teeth at the skin. Anticipation.
Then flesh. Grain on the tongue.
Eve's knees ground in the dirt
of paradise. Newton watching
gravity happen. The history
of apples in each starry core,
every papery chamber's bright
bitter seed. Woody stem
an infant tree. William Tell
and his lucky arrow. Orchards
of the Fertile Crescent. Bushels.
Fire blight. Scab and powdery mildew.
Cedar apple rust. The apple endures.
Born on the wild rose, of crab ancestors.
The first pip raised in Kazakhstan.
Snow White with poison on her lips.
The buried blades of Halloween.
Budding and grafting. John Chapman
in his tin pot hat. Oh Westward
Expansion. Apple pie. American
as. Hard cider. Winter banana.
Melt-in-the-mouth made sweet
by hives of Britain's honeybees:
white man's flies. O eat. O eat.

Hunger

JACK GILBERT

Digging into the apple
with my thumbs.
Scraping out the closed nails
and digging deeper.
Refusing the moon color.
Refusing the smell and memories.
Digging in with the sweet juice
running along my hands unpleasantly.
Refusing the sweetness.
Turning my hands to gouge out chunks.
Feeling the juice sticky
on my wrists. The skin itching.
Getting to the wooden part.
Getting to the seeds.
Going on.
Not taking anyone's word for it.
Getting beyond the seeds.

Collards

JAMES APPLEWHITE

Green hens perching the pole
      Of a row, concentric wings
Fly you down into soil.

You catch the rain like rings
      Where a pine stump tunnels
Time backward down roots' seasonings.

If roots rot to dark channels
      Mining the forest, your fiber
Threads grease in the entrails

Of families, whose bodies harbor
      Scars like rain on a hillslope,
Whose skin takes sheen like lumber

Left out in the weather. Old folk
      Seem sewed together by pulp
Of your green rope and smoke

From the cook fires boys gulp
      For dinner along roads in winter.
Collards and ham grease they drop

In the pot come back as we enter
      The house whose porch shows a pumpkin.
This steam holds all we remember.

Sweet potatoes clot in a bin,
     Common flesh beneath this skin
Like collards. Grainy-sweet, kin.

cutting greens

LUCILLE CLIFTON

curling them around
i hold their bodies in obscene embrace
thinking of everything but kinship.
collards and kale
strain against each strange other
away from my kissmaking hand and
the iron bedpot.
the pot is black,
the cutting board is black,
my hand,
and just for a minute
the greens roll black under the knife,
and the kitchen twists dark on its spine
and i taste in my natural appetite
the bond of live things everywhere.

GIVING THANKS

*Oyster stuffing, for turkeys naturally, is as American as corn-on-the-cob
or steamed coot, as far as Americans know or care. To many families it is
a necessary part of Christmas dinner, so that its omission would at once
connotate a sure sign of internal disintegration, as if Ma came to church in her
corset-cover or Uncle Jim brought his light-o'-love to the children's picnic.*

—M. F. K. FISHER

"A LUSTY BIT OF NOURISHMENT"

Oysters

SEAMUS HEANEY

Our shells clacked on the plates.
My tongue was a filling estuary,
My palate hung with starlight:
As I tasted the salty Pleiades
Orion dipped his foot into the water.

Alive and violated
They lay on their beds of ice:
Bivalves: the split bulb
And philandering sigh of ocean.
Millions of them ripped and shucked and scattered.

We had driven to that coast
Through flowers and limestone
And there we were, toasting friendship,
Laying down a perfect memory
In the cool of thatch and crockery.

Over the Alps, packed deep in hay and snow,
The Romans hauled their oysters south to Rome:
I saw damp panniers disgorge
The frond-lipped, brine-stung
Glut of privilege

And was angry that my trust could not repose
In the clear light, like poetry or freedom
Leaning in from sea. I ate the day
Deliberately, that its tang
Might quicken me all into verb, pure verb.

Invocation, 1926

NATASHA TRETHEWEY

for Loretta Dixon Turnbough

How they rose early, a list of chores
pulling them toward the kitchen
in dim light—work that must be done
before the rest of their work be done.

How they walked for miles, down
the Gulf and Ship Island Line, toward
the beach, through the quarters, beyond
shotgun shacks, and into the city limits

where white children stood guard—sentries
on a section of rail—muscling them off
the tracks. How they walked on, anyway,
until they waded into water, neck-deep—

though they could not swim—a baptism,
something akin to faith, the daily catch
keeping them afloat. How they tied the lines,
walked back and forth to find each cluster,

each glorious net of crabs. Across sand, roads
hot beneath their feet, then door to back door
they went, my grandmother and her siblings,
knocking, offering their catch, cleaned first

on the back steps, gutted—a display of yellow
bright as sunshine raining down on the grass.
When my grandmother prepared crabs for me
I could see the girl she was, her nimble hands,

food on the table in all those alien houses
along the beach. On our table: gumbo manna,
rice steaming in a bowl; the communion
between us and them—the white folks

across the tracks—sure as the crab lines she set,
the work of her hands, that which sustains us.
Lord, bless those hands, the harvesters. Bless
the travelers who gather our food, and those

who grow it, clean it, cook it, who bring it
to our tables. Bless the laborers whose faces
we do not see—like the girl my grandmother was,
walking the rails home; bless us that we remember.

The Fish

ELIZABETH BISHOP

I caught a tremendous fish
and held him beside the boat
half out of water, with my hook
fast in a corner of his mouth.
He didn't fight.
He hadn't fought at all.
He hung a grunting weight,
battered and venerable
and homely. Here and there
his brown skin hung in strips
like ancient wallpaper,
and its pattern of darker brown
was like wallpaper:
shapes like full-blown roses
stained and lost through age.
He was speckled with barnacles,
fine rosettes of lime,
and infested
with tiny white sea-lice,
and underneath two or three
rags of green weed hung down.
While his gills were breathing in
the terrible oxygen
—the frightening gills,
fresh and crisp with blood,
that can cut so badly—
I thought of the coarse white flesh

packed in like feathers,
the big bones and the little bones,
the dramatic reds and blacks
of his shiny entrails,
and the pink swim-bladder
like a big peony.
I looked into his eyes
which were far larger than mine
but shallower, and yellowed,
the irises backed and packed
with tarnished tinfoil
seen through the lenses
of old scratched isinglass.
They shifted a little, but not
to return my stare.
—It was more like the tipping
of an object toward the light.
I admired his sullen face,
the mechanism of his jaw,
and then I saw
that from his lower lip
—if you could call it a lip—
grim, wet, and weaponlike,
hung five old pieces of fish-line,
or four and a wire leader
with the swivel still attached,
with all their five big hooks
grown firmly in his mouth.
A green line, frayed at the end
where he broke it, two heavier lines,
and a fine black thread
still crimped from the strain and snap
when it broke and he got away.
Like medals with their ribbons

frayed and wavering,
a five-haired beard of wisdom
trailing from his aching jaw.
I stared and stared
and victory filled up
the little rented boat,
from the pool of bilge
where oil had spread a rainbow
around the rusted engine
to the bailer rusted orange,
the sun-cracked thwarts,
the oarlocks on their strings,
the gunnels—until everything
was rainbow, rainbow, rainbow!
And I let the fish go.

A Display of Mackerel

MARK DOTY

They lie in parallel rows,
on ice, head to tail,
each a foot of luminosity

barred with black bands,
which divide the scales'
radiant sections

like seams of lead
in a Tiffany window.
Iridescent, watery

prismatics: think abalone,
the wildly rainbowed
mirror of a soapbubble sphere,

think sun on gasoline.
Splendor, and splendor,
and not a one in any way

distinguished from the other
—nothing about them
of individuality. Instead

they're *all* exact expressions
of the one soul,
each a perfect fulfilment

of heaven's template,
mackerel essence. As if,
after a lifetime arriving

at this enameling, the jeweler's
made uncountable examples,
each as intricate

in its oily fabulation
as the one before.
Suppose we could iridesce,

like these, and lose ourselves
entirely in the universe
of shimmer—would you want

to be yourself only,
unduplicatable, doomed
to be lost? They'd prefer,

plainly, to be flashing participants,
multitudinous. Even now
they seem to be bolting

forward, heedless of stasis.
They don't care they're dead
and nearly frozen,

just as, presumably,
they didn't care that they were living:
all, all for all,

the rainbowed school
and its acres of brilliant classrooms,
in which no verb is singular,

or every one is. How happy they seem,
even on ice, to be together, selfless,
which is the price of gleaming.

The Fish

BILLY COLLINS

As soon as the elderly waiter
placed before me the fish I had ordered,
it began to stare up at me
with its one flat, iridescent eye.

I feel sorry for you, it seemed to say,
eating alone in this awful restaurant
bathed in such unkindly light
and surrounded by these dreadful murals of Sicily.

And I feel sorry for you, too—
yanked from the sea and now lying dead
next to some boiled potatoes in Pittsburgh—
I said back to the fish as I raised my fork.

And thus my dinner in an unfamiliar city
with its rivers and lighted bridges
was graced not only with chilled wine
and lemon slices but with compassion and sorrow

even after the waiter removed my plate
with the head of the fish still staring
and the barrel vault of its delicate bones
terribly exposed, save for a shroud of parsley.

Four Sonnets About Food

ADRIENNE SU

1
Words can't do
what bird bones
can: stew
to the stony
essence
of one
small soul, the spent
sacrifice boiled down
to the hard white
matter that nourishes
the mighty
predator, who flourishes
on the slaughtered
animal and water.

2
Who feeds
another is like bones
to him who eats
(I say "him" only
because it is a man
in my house
who eats and a woman
who goes about
the matter of sustenance),
food being always
a matter of life and

death and each day's
dining
another small dying.

3
Scallops seared
in hot iron
with grated ginger,
rice wine,
and a little oil
of sesame, served
with boiled
jasmine rice, cures
the malaise
of long, fluorescent
weekdays
spent
in the city
for money.

4
I am afraid
I can't always be
here when you need
a warm body
or words; someday
I'll slip
into the red clay
I started with
and forget
who you are,
but
for now, here's
my offering: baked red
fish, clear soup, bread.

Farm Country

MARY OLIVER

I have sharpened my knives, I have
Put on the heavy apron.

Maybe you think life is chicken soup, served
In blue willow-pattern bowls.

I have put on my boots and opened
The kitchen door and stepped out

Into the sunshine. I have crossed the lawn,
I have entered

The hen house.

Ode to Chicken

KEVIN YOUNG

You are everything
to me. Frog legs,
rattlesnake, almost any
thing I put my mouth to
reminds me of you.
Folks always try
getting you to act
like you someone else—
nuggets, or tenders, fingers
you don't have—but even
your unmanicured feet
taste sweet. Too loud
in the yard, segregated
dark & light, you are
like a day self-contained—
your sunset skin puckers
like a kiss. Let others
put on airs—pigs graduate
to pork, bread
becomes toast, even beef
was once just bull
before it got them degrees—
but, even dead,
you keep your name
& head. You can make
anything of yourself,
you know—but prefer

to wake me early
in the cold, fix me breakfast
& dinner too, leave me
to fly for you.

The Thanksgivings

HARRIET MAXWELL CONVERSE

We who are here present thank the Great Spirit that we are here to
    praise Him.
We thank Him that He has created men and women, and ordered that
    these beings shall always be living to multiply the earth.
We thank Him for making the earth and giving these beings its
    products to live on.
We thank Him for the water that comes out of the earth and runs for
    our lands.
We thank Him for all the animals on the earth.
We thank Him for certain timbers that grow and have fluids coming
    from them for us all.
We thank Him for the branches of the trees that grow shadows for our
    shelter.
We thank Him for the beings that come from the west, the thunder
    and lightning that water the earth.
We thank Him for the light which we call our oldest brother, the sun
    that works for our good.
We thank Him for all the fruits that grow on the trees and vines.
We thank Him for his goodness in making the forests, and thank all
    its trees.
We thank Him for the darkness that gives us rest, and for the kind
    Being of the darkness that gives us light, the moon.
We thank Him for the bright spots in the skies that give us signs, the
    stars.
We give Him thanks for our supporters, who had charge of our
    harvests.

We give Him thanks that the voice of the Great Spirit can still be
heard through the words of Ga-ne-o-di-o.
We thank the Great Spirit that we have the privilege of this pleasant
occasion.
We give thanks for the persons who can sing the Great Spirit's music,
and hope they will be privileged to continue in his faith.
We thank the Great Spirit for all the persons who perform the
ceremonics on this occasion.

Translated from a traditional Iroquois prayer

What They Ate

CAMPBELL MCGRATH

All manner of fowl and wild game: venison, raccoon, opossum,
    turkey.
Abundant fishes, excepting salmon, which ws. found distasteful.
Meat of all sorts, especially pig, which roamed free and was fatty.
Also shellfish: quahogs and foot-long oysters; lobsters, though
    considered wasteful.

Wild fruit: huckle and rasp, blue being known as "skycolored"
    berries.
Parsnips, turnips, carrots, onions: these sown loosely and rooted out;
while these were cultivated in orchards: apples, peaches, apricots,
    cherries.
Cabbage—favored by the Dutch as *koolslaa*, by the Germans as
    sauerkraut—

was boiled with herbs brought from England; thyme, hyssop,
    marjoram, parsley.
Pumpkin, dried, or mashed with butter, where yams grew sparsely.
Corn, with beans as *succotash*; called *samp* when milled to grist;
in the South, hulled and broken, as *hominy*; or fried with bacon
    as grits.
Maple ws. not favored; loaves of white sugar worth considerable
    money
were kept under lock, cut with special sugar shears. For honey,

bees were imported, called "English flies" by the Narragansett.

My Days Are Numbered

RICK MORANIS

The average American home now has more television sets than people . . .
according to Nielsen Media Research. There are 2.73 TV sets
in the typical home and 2.55 people, the researchers said.

THE ASSOCIATED PRESS, SEPT. 21.

I have two kids. Both are away at college.

I have five television sets. (I like to think of them as a set of five
televisions.) I have two DVR boxes, three DVD players, two
VHS machines and four stereos.

I have nineteen remote controls, mostly in one drawer.

I have three computers, four printers and two non working faxes.

I have three phone lines, three cell phones and two answering
machines.

I have no messages.

I have forty-six cookbooks.

I have sixty-eight takeout menus from four restaurants.

I have one hundred and sixteen soy sauce packets.

I have three hundred and eighty-two dishes, bowls, cups, saucers, mugs and glasses.

I eat over the sink.

I have five sinks, two with a view.

I try to keep a positive view.

I have two refrigerators.

It's very hard to count ice cubes.

I have thirty-nine pairs of golf, tennis, squash, running, walking, hiking, casual and formal shoes, ice skates and rollerblades.

I'm wearing slippers.

I have forty-one 37-cent stamps.

I have no 2-cent stamps.

I read three dailies, four weeklies, five monthlies and no annual reports.

I have five hundred and six CD, cassette, vinyl and eight-track recordings.

I listen to the same radio station all day.

I have twenty-six sets of linen for four regular, three foldout and two inflatable beds.

I don't like having houseguests.

I have one hundred and eighty-four thousand frequent flier miles on
six airlines, three of which no longer exist.

I have "101 Dalmatians" on tape.

I have fourteen digital clocks flashing relatively similar times.

I have twenty-two minutes to listen to the news.

I have nine armchairs from which I can be critical.

I have a laundry list of things that need cleaning.

I have lost more than one thousand golf balls.

I am missing thirty-seven umbrellas.

I have over four hundred yards of dental floss.

I have a lot of time on my hands.

I have two kids coming home for Thanksgiving.

First Thanksgiving

SHARON OLDS

When she comes back, from college, I will see
the skin of her upper arms, cool,
matte, glossy. She will hug me, my old
soupy chest against her breasts,
I will smell her hair! She will sleep in this apartment,
her sleep like an untamed, good object, like a
soul in a body. She came into my life the
second great arrival, fresh
from the other world—which lay, from within him,
within me. Those nights, I fed her to sleep,
week after week, the moon rising,
and setting, and waxing—whirling, over the months,
in a steady blur, around our planet.
Now she doesn't need love like that, she has
had it. She will walk in glowing, we will talk,
and then, when she's fast asleep, I'll exult
to have her in that room again,
behind that door! As a child, I caught
bees, by the wings, and held them, some seconds,
looked into their wild faces,
listened to them sing, then tossed them back
into the air—I remember the moment the
arc of my toss swerved, and they entered
the corrected curve of their departure.

CHURNING & PRESERVING

If you're afraid of butter, use cream.

—JULIA CHILD

Butter

ELIZABETH ALEXANDER

My mother loves butter more than I do,
more than anyone. She pulls chunks off
the stick and eats it plain, explaining
cream spun around into butter! Growing up
we ate turkey cutlets sauteed in lemon
and butter, butter and cheese on green noodles,
butter melting in small pools in the hearts
of Yorkshire puddings, butter better
than gravy staining white rice yellow,
butter glazing corn in slipping squares,
butter the lava in white volcanoes
of hominy grits, butter softening
in a white bowl to be creamed with white
sugar, butter disappearing into
whipped potatoes, with pineapple,
butter melted and curdy to pour
over pancakes, butter licked off the plate
with warm Alaga syrup. When I picture
the good old days I am grinning greasy
with my brother, having watched the tiger
chase his tail and turn to butter. We are
Mumbo and Jumbo's children despite
historical revision, despite
our parent's efforts, glowing from the inside
out, one hundred megawatts of butter.

Ode to Butter

LINTON HOPKINS

Thou still unravished bride of promises
a child of art and craft
fixed with many suitors eyes
born of Thracia from capra and aries
reaching perfection with the taurus

Vollon, still life's master
conjured you in 1875
Escoffier's contemporary, he knew who you were:
a foundation.

In ancient India you were clarified into one of their most elemental
        of foods.
GHEE, Sanskrit for "bright"
you are an ancient offering to the gods and burned in holy lamps and
        funeral pyres
eternal

beaten out of cream
kneaded and shaped
salted to preserve
fresh, room temp—there is no need to refrigerate you
as the poet Seamus said
you are "coagulated sunlight"

sunlight transformed by the cow
from the seasonal hue

cool and spreadable I taste your season,
bright, fat and herbal in spring and summer when
fed on clover and fresh grass
in the winter you taste of hay and grain

Julia became Julia when met with your aroma
commingling in a pan with shallots
many people don't know that you actually lighten a dish
small knobs stirred into reduced stock
mouthfeel, richness
the dish which is missing something
is quickly set right

Would French cuisine exist without you?
Chef Point in '37, manned the stoves at La Pyramide writing
"Butter! Give me Butter! Always Butter!"

So versatile are you
clarified to remove the milk
you saute at high heat
whole at low flame you perform a feat of magic:
you emulsify with yourself
the water, milk solids and fat,
a whisk, some coaxing
a smooth warm sauce is born, beurre monte
a little wine vinegar and shallot . . . beurre blanc

toasted till hazelnut brown; noisette
darkened to almost burnt dark black; noir
worked into eggs: hollandaise and bernaise

asparagus, broccoli, and legumes
they all cry out for you

Pastry without you is unimaginable
your melting between the million layers is the puff
pate brisee, pate sucree,
cookies and cakes all begin with creaming
you and sugar

the South?
fresh churned from cream with a second gift; buttermilk
whose quality is determined by how many of your children float
        across the surface
spread on warm biscuits with sorghum
a small knob in a bowl of grits
steaming hot sweet potatoes with you on top
bread & butter pickles tell us how they should be eaten
sweet, sour and unctuous
butterbeans are named in your honor
creamy like you when cooked right
glazed with you and black pepper
memories.

Who has not thought of you when you are not around?
hungry and romantic
blamed for a multitude of sins
doctors who decry you are often found at your back door
new science has shown;
you ain't all that bad.
in fact, your very nature may be good for the fabric of our brain
I knew that already

Think not of others.
Margarine, unworthy imitation, it has no song
Lard, Schmaltz Oil.
they are not so universal
nor so simple and complex
an infinite story

I place you in an ancestral black iron pan
watch you glaze across the black surface
when the bubbles foam and begin to subside
it is an invitation

add the minced onions and sweat
the beginning of so many journeys
from gumbo to perloo
I always begin with you

American Milk

RUTH STONE

Then the butter we put on our white bread
was colored with butter yellow, a cancerous dye,
and all the fourth grades were taken by streetcar
to the Dunky Company to see milk processed; milk bottles
riding on narrow metal cogs through little doors that flapped.
The sour damp smell of milky-wet cement floors:
we looked through great glass windows at the milk.
Before we were herded back to the streetcar line,
we were each given a half pint of milk in tiny
milk bottles with straws to suck it up. In this way
we gradually learned about our country.

Sad Verso of the Sunny___

LIZ WALDNER

Veldt? Sounds good to me.
Like melt. Back when you could eat Velveeta
and call it cheese. My grandfather's macaroni and cheese
featured a whole brick of Velveeta. I liked peeling away
its beautiful silver wrapper, *Velveeta Velveeta* all over in blue.

The expanses of time in which there was this grandfather
appeared endless when I was in them. Who
could see to the ends of the plains and so see her end
beyond them? Who could think to look? You
(like Ohio and its vowels) went on forever,
just ate your macaroni and cheese, relishing
the brown bubbles on top, then did the next thing,
were the next moment surrounded and held in it
by all the things you didn't know would end.
Nothing ceded. No portend.
Only geranium and melamine
and thank you,
everywhere preceded by some please.

The Butter Factory

LES MURRAY

It was built of things that must not mix:
paint, cream and water, fire and dusty oil.
You heard the water dreaming in its large
kneed pipes, up from the weir. And the cordwood
our fathers cut for the furnace stood in walls
like the sleeper-stacks of a continental railway.

The cream arrived in lorried tides; its procession
crossed a platform of workers' stagecraft: *Come here
Friday-Legs! Or I'll feel your hernia—*
Overalled in milk's colour, men moved the heart of milk,
separated into thousands, along a roller track—*Trucks?
That one of mine, son, it pulls like a sixteen-year-old—*
to the tester who broached the can lids, causing fat tears,
who tasted, dipped and did his thin stoppered chemistry
on our labour, as the empties chattered downstage and fumed.

Under the high roof, black-crusted and stainless steels
were walled apart. black romped with leather belts
but paddlewheels sailed the silvery vats where muscles
of the one deep cream were exercised to a bullion
to be blocked in paper. And between waves of delivery
the men trod on water, hosing the rainbows of a shift.

It was damp April even at Christmas round every
margin of the factory. Also it opened the mouth
to see tackles on glibbed gravel, and the mossed char louvres

of the ice-plant's timber tower streaming with
heavy rain all day, above the droughty paddocks
of the totem cows round whom our lives were dancing.

O Cheese

DONALD HALL

In the pantry the dear dense cheeses, Cheddars and harsh
Lancashires; Gorgonzola with its magnanimous manner;
the clipped speech of Roquefort; and a head of Stilton
that speaks in a sensuous riddling tongue like Druids.

O cheeses of gravity, cheeses of wistfulness, cheeses
that weep continually because they know they will die.
O cheeses of victory, cheeses wise in defeat, cheeses
fat as a cushion, lolling in bed until noon.

Liederkranz ebullient, jumping like a small dog, noisy;
Pont l'Évêque intellectual, and quite well informed; Emmentaler
decent and loyal, a little deaf in the right ear;
and Brie the revealing experience, instantaneous and profound.

O cheeses that dance in the moonlight, cheeses
that mingle with sausages, cheeses of Stonehenge.
O cheeses that are shy, that linger in the doorway,
eyes looking down, cheeses spectacular as fireworks.

Reblochon openly sexual; Caerphilly like pine trees, small
at the timberline; Port-du-Salut in love; Camembert
eloquent, tactful, like a thousand-year-old hostess;
and Dolcelatte, always generous to a fault.

O village of cheeses, I make you this poem of cheeses,
O family of cheeses, living together in pantries,
O cheeses that keep to your own nature, like a lucky couple,
this solitude, this energy, these bodies slowly dying.

Applesauce

TED KOOSER

I liked how the starry blue lid
of that saucepan lifted and puffed,
then settled back on a thin
hotpad of steam, and the way
her kitchen filled with the warm,
wet breath of apples, as if all
the apples were talking at once,
as if they'd come cold and sour
from chores in the orchard,
and were trying to shoulder in
close to the fire. She was too busy
to put in her two cents' worth
talking to apples. Squeezing
her dentures with wrinkly lips,
she had to jingle and stack
the bright brass coins of the lids
and thoughtfully count out
the red rubber rings, then hold
each jar, to see if it was clean,
to a window that looked out
through her back yard into Iowa.
And with every third or fourth jar
she wiped steam from her glasses,
using the hem of her apron,
printed with tiny red sailboats
that dipped along with leaf-green
banners snapping, under puffs

of pale applesauce clouds
scented with cinnamon and cloves,
the only boats under sail
for at least two thousand miles.

The Preserving

KEVIN YOUNG

Summer meant peeling: peaches,
pears, July, all carved up. August
was a tomato dropped
in boiling water, my skin coming
right off. And peas, Lord,
after shelling all summer, if I never
saw those green fingers again
it would be too soon. We'd also
make wine, gather up those peach
scraps, put them in jars & let them
turn. Trick was enough air.

Eating something boiled each meal,
my hair in coils by June first, Mama
could barely reel me in from the red
clay long enough to wrap my hair
with string. So tight
I couldn't think. But that was far
easier to take care of, lasted all
summer like ashy knees.
One Thanksgiving, while saying grace
we heard what sounded like a gunshot
ran to the back porch to see
peach glass everywhere. Reckon
someone didn't give the jar enough

room to breathe. Only good thing
bout them saving days was knowing
they'd be over, that by Christmas
afternoons turned to cakes: coconut
yesterday, fruitcake today, fresh
cushaw pie to start tomorrow.
On Jesus' Day we'd go house
to house tasting each family's peach
brandy. You know you could stand
only so much, a taste. Time we weaved
back, it had grown cold as war.
Huddling home, clutching each
other in our handed down hand-
me-downs, we felt we was dying
like a late fire; we prayed
those homemade spirits
would warm most way home.

Root Cellar

THEODORE ROETHKE

Nothing would sleep in that cellar, dank as a ditch,
Bulbs broke out of boxes hunting for chinks in the dark,
Shoots dangled and drooped,
Lolling obscenely from mildewed crates,
Hung down long yellow evil necks, like tropical snakes.
And what a congress of stinks!—
Roots ripe as old bait,
Pulpy stems, rank, silo-rich,
Leaf-mold, manure, lime, piled against slippery planks.
Nothing would give up life:
Even the dirt kept breathing a small breath.

Refrigerator, 1957

THOMAS LUX

More like a vault—you pull the handle out
and on the shelves: not a lot,
and what there is (a boiled potato
in a bag, a chicken carcass
under foil) looking dispirited,
drained, mugged. This is not
a place to go in hope or hunger.
But, just to the right of the middle
of the middle door shelf, on fire, a lit-from-within red,
heart red, sexual red, wet neon red,
shining red in their liquid, exotic,
aloof, slumming
in such company: a jar
of maraschino cherries. Three-quarters
full, fiery globes, like strippers
at a church social. Maraschino cherries, maraschino,
the only foreign word I knew. Not once
did I see these cherries employed: not
in a drink, nor on top
of a glob of ice cream,
or just pop one in your mouth. Not once.
The same jar there through an entire
childhood of dull dinners—bald meat,
pocked peas and, see above,
boiled potatoes. Maybe
they came over from the old country,
family heirlooms, or were status symbols

bought with a piece of the first paycheck
from a sweatshop,
which beat the pig farm in Bohemia,
handed down from my grandparents
to my parents
to be someday mine,
then my child's?
They were beautiful
and, if I never ate one,
it was because I knew it might be missed
or because I knew it would not be replaced
and because you do not eat
that which rips your heart with joy.

II.
Wintering

Them belly full but we hungry.
—BOB MARLEY

SOUP LINES & STAPLES

*There are people in the world so hungry, that God
cannot appear to them except in the form of bread.*
—MAHATMA GANDHI

Te Deum

CHARLES REZNIKOFF

Not because of victories
I sing,
having none,
but for the common sunshine,
the breeze,
the largess of the spring.

Not for victory
but for the day's work done
as well as I was able;
not for a seat upon the dais
but at the common table.

I, Too, Sing America

LANGSTON HUGHES

I, too, sing America.

I am the darker brother.
They send me to eat in the kitchen
When company comes,
But I laugh,
And eat well,
And grow strong.

Tomorrow,
I'll be at the table
When company comes.
Nobody'll dare
Say to me,
"Eat in the kitchen,"
Then.

Besides,
They'll see how beautiful I am
And be ashamed—

I, too, am America.

To a Poor Old Woman

WILLIAM CARLOS WILLIAMS

munching a plum on
the street a paper bag
of them in her hand

They taste good to her
They taste good
to her. They taste
good to her

You can see it by
the way she gives herself
to the one half
sucked out in her hand

Comforted
a solace of ripe plums
seeming to fill the air
They taste good to her

At the IGA: Franklin, New Hampshire

JANE KENYON

This is where I would shop
if my husband worked felling trees
for the mill, hurting himself badly
from time to time; where I would bring
my three kids; where I would push
one basket and pull another
because the boxes of diapers and cereal
and gallon milk jugs take so much room.

I would already have put the clothes
in the two largest washers next door
at the Norge Laundry Village. Done shopping,
I'd pile the wet wash in trash bags
and take it home to dry on the line.

And I would think, hanging out the baby's
shirts and sleepers, and cranking the pulley
away from me, how it would be
to change lives with someone,
like the woman who came after us
in the checkout, thin, with lots of rings
on her hands, who looked us over openly.

Things would have been different
if I hadn't let Bob climb on top of me
for ninety seconds in 1979.
It was raining lightly in the state park

and so we were alone. The charcoal fire
hissed as the first drops fell. . . .
In ninety seconds we made this life—

a trailer on a windy hill, dangerous jobs
in the woods or night work at the packing plant;
Roy, Kimberly, Bobby; too much in the hamper,
never enough in the bank.

Economics at Gemco

JOHN OLIVARES ESPINOZA

My mother pushes a grocery cart,
I tug at her blue pleated skirt.

She puts her change into my hands,
For the old soul slumped against the wall,
His gray mouth covered by a beard of wind and dirt.

I place the coins into his cupped hands
And he stacks two neat columns of cents
Next to his seat on the curb.
He nods his chin half-solemnly.

I turn back to Mother,
Suddenly a cop—he came out of nowhere—
Tells me, *Take the money back.*
I brush the coins
Back into my palms like table crumbs.
As the old man,
Silent as those pennies,
Gets cuffed and hauled off to jail.
I ask Mom why—
We only tried to help.

The cop says bums make thirty bucks a week
Begging for change
And are not too unhappy
When arrested

Since they get food, shelter,
And a hot shower for at least a week.

My mother pushes the grocery cart without a word,
Knowing that as newlyweds she begged outside markets for change
While Dad stole bread and sliced honey-ham inside.

The Saint Vincent de Paul
Food Pantry Stomp

MARTÍN ESPADA

Madison, Wisconsin, 1980

Waiting for the carton of food
given with Christian suspicion
even to agency-certified charity cases
like me,
thin and brittle
as uncooked linguini,
anticipating the factory-damaged cans
of tomato soup, beets, three-bean salad
in a welfare cornucopia,
I spotted a squashed dollar bill
on the floor, and with
a Saint Vincent de Paul food pantry stomp
pinned it under my sneaker,
tied my laces meticulously,
and stuffed the bill in my sock
like a smuggler of diamonds,
all beneath the plaster statue wingspan
of Saint Vinnie,
who was unaware
of the dance
named in his honor
by a maraca shaker
in the salsa band
of the unemployed.

Capitalist Poem #5

CAMPBELL MCGRATH

I was at the 7-11.
I ate a burrito.
I drank a Slurpee.
I was tired.
It was late, after work—washing dishes.
The burrito was good.
I had another.

I did it every day for a week.
I did it every day for a month.

To cook a burrito you tear off the plastic wrapper.
You push button #3 on the microwave.
Burritos are large, small, or medium.
Red or green chili peppers.
Beef or bean or both.
There are 7-11's all across the nation.

On the way out I bought a quart of beer for $1.39.
I was aware of social injustice

in only the vaguest possible way.

Sugar

YUSEF KOMUNYAKAA

I watched men at Angola,
How every swing of the machete
Swelled the day black with muscles,
Like a wave through canestalks,
Pushed by the eyes of guards
Who cradled pump shotguns like lovers.
They swayed to a Cuban samba or Yoruba
Master drum & wrote confessions in the air
Saying *I been wrong*
But I'll be right someday
I gazed from Lorenzo's '52 Chevy
Till they were nighthawks,
& days later fell asleep
Listening to Cousin Buddy's
One-horse mill grind out a blues.
We fed stalks into metal jaws
That locked in sweetness
When everything cooled down & crusted over,
Leaving only a few horseflies
To buzz & drive the day beyond
Leadbelly. At the bottom
Of each gallon was a glacier,
A fetish I could buy a kiss with.
I stared at a tree against dusk
Till it was a girl
Standing beside a country road
Shucking cane with her teeth.

She looked up & smiled
& waved. Lost in what hurts,
In what tasted good, could she
Ever learn there's no love
In sugar?

Sherbet

CORNELIUS EADY

The problem here is that
This isn't pretty, the
Sort of thing that

Can easily be dealt with
With words. After
All it's

A horror story to sit,
A black man with
A white wife in

The middle of a hot
Sunday afternoon in
The Jefferson Hotel in

Richmond, Va., and wait
Like a criminal for service
From a young white waitress

Who has decided that
This looks like something
She doesn't want

To be a part of. What poetry
Could describe the
Perfect angle of

This woman's back as
She walks, just so,
Mapping the room off

Like the end of a
Border dispute, which
Metaphor could turn

The room more perfectly
Into a group of
Islands? And when

The manager finally
Arrives, what language
Do I use

To translate the nervous
Eye motions, the yawning
Afternoon silence, the

Prayer beneath
His simple inquiries,
The sherbet which

He then brings to the table personally,
Just to be certain
The doubt

Stays on our side
Of the fence? What do
We call the rich,

Sweet taste of
Frozen oranges in
This context? What do

We call a weight that
Doesn't fingerprint,
Won't shift,

And can't explode?

Appetite

TRACY K. SMITH

It's easy to understand that girl's father
Telling her it's time to come in and eat.
Because the food is good and hot.
Because he has worked all day
In the same shirt, unbuttoned now
With its dirty neck and a patch
With his name on the chest.

The girl is not hungry enough
To go in. She has spent all day
Indoors playing on rugs, making her eyes
See rooms and houses where there is only
Shadow and light. She knows
That she knows nothing of the world,
Which makes the stoop where she kneels
So difficult to rise from.

But her father is ready to stuff himself
On mashed potatoes and sliced bread,
Ready to raise a leg of chicken to his lips,
Then a wing; to feel the heat enter through his teeth,
Skin giving way like nothing else
Will give way to him in this lifetime.

He's ready to take a bite
Of the pink tomatoes while his mouth
Is still full with something else,

To hurry it down his throat
With a swig of beer, shrugging
When his wife says, *You're setting
A bad example*. It doesn't matter—

Too many eyes without centers
For one day. Too many
Dice, cards, dogs with faces like sharks
Tethered to chains. It gives him
An empty feeling below his stomach,
And all he can think to call it
Is appetite. And so he will lie
When he kisses his napkin and says
Hits the spot, as his daughter will lie
When she learns to parrot him,
Not yet knowing what her own appetite
Points to.

The Bean Eaters

GWENDOLYN BROOKS

They eat beans mostly, this old yellow pair.
Dinner is a casual affair.
Plain chipware on a plain and creaking wood,
Tin flatware.

Two who are Mostly Good.
Two who have lived their day,
But keep on putting on their clothes
And putting things away.

And remembering . . .
Remembering with twinklings and twinges,
As they lean over the beans in their rented back room that
  is full of beads and receipts and dolls and cloths,
  tobacco crumbs, vases and fringes.

The Broad Bean Sermon

LES MURRAY

Beanstalks, in any breeze, are a slack church parade
without belief, saying *trespass against us* in unison,
recruits in mint Air Force Dacron, with unbuttoned leaves.

Upright with water like men, square in stem-section
they grow to great lengths, drink rain, keel over all ways,
kink down and grow up afresh, with proffered new greenstuff.

Above the cat-and-mouse floor of a thin bean forest
snails hang rapt in their food, ants hurry through several dimensions:
spiders tense and sag like little black flags in their cordage.

Going out to pick beans with the sun high as fence-tops, you find
plenty, and fetch them. An hour or a cloud later
you find shirtfulls more. At every hour of daylight

appear more than you missed: ripe, knobbly ones, fleshy-sided,
thin-straight, thin-crescent, frown shaped, bird-shouldered, boat-
        keeled ones.
beans knuckled and single-bulged, minute green dolphins at suck,

beans upright like lecturing, outstretched like blessing fingers
in the incident light, and more still, oblique to your notice
that the noon glare or cloud-light or afternoon slants will uncover

till you ask yourself Could I have overlooked so many, or
do they form in an hour? unfolding into reality
like templates for subtly broad grins, like unique caught expressions,

like edible meanings, each sealed around with a string
and affixed to its moment, an unceasing colloquial assembly,
the portly, the stiff, and those lolling in pointed green slippers . . .

Wondering who'll take the spare bagfulls, you grin with happiness
—it is your health—you vow to pick them all
even the last few, weeks off yet, misshapen as toes.

Beans: An Apologia for Not Loving to Cook

JUDITH ORTIZ COFER

for Tanya

For me memory turns on the cloying smell of boiling beans
in a house of women waiting, waiting for wars, affairs, periods
of grieving, the rains, *el mal tiempo*, to end, the phrase
used both for inclement weather and to abbreviate the aftermath
of personal tragedies. And they waited for beans to boil.
My grandmother would put a pot on the slow fire
at dawn, and all day long, the stones she had dropped in, hard
and dry as a betrayed woman's eyes, slowly softened, scenting
the house with the essence of waiting. Beans.
I grew to hate them.
Red kidney beans whose name echoes of blood, and that are shaped
like inner organs, I hated them in their jaw-breaking rawness
and I hated them as they yielded to the fire.

The women waited in turns by the stove
rapt by the alchemy of unmaking. The mothers turned hard
at the stove, resisting our calls with the ultimate threat
of burned beans. The vigil made them statues, rivulets
of sweat coursing down their faces, pooling at their collarbones.
They turned hard away from our demands for attention and love,
their eyes and hands making sure beans would not burn
and rice would not stick, unaware of our longing
for our mothers' spirits to return back to the soft sac
that once held us, safely tucked among their inner organs,
smelling the beans they cooked for others,
through their pores.

The beans took half a child's lifetime to cook,
and when they were ready to bring to table
in soup bowls, the women called the men first
in high voices like whistles pitched above our range,
food offered like sacred, steaming sacrifice to *los hombres*.
El hambre entered the room with them, hunger
as a special presence, called forth from whatever other realm
the women visited when they cooked, their bodies
remaining on earth to watch the beans
while they flew away from us for hours.

                                        As others fed
I watched the dog at the screen door, legs trembling,
who whimpered and waited for the scrap. I hated
the growling of pleasure when at last it got its gory bone
I resisted the lessons of the kitchen then, fearing
the Faustian exchanges of adults, the shape-shifting nature
of women by the fire.

Now it is my daughter who keeps a voluntary vigil by the stove.
She loves the idea of cooking as chemistry, and the Tao
of making food. Her waiting for the beans to boil is a meditation
on the transformative properties of matter; a gift of memory food
from my island. And I come out of my poem to partake, to share
her delight in the art of feeding, like a recently freed captive
of a long-ago war, capable at last of a peaceful surrender
to my old nemesis, *el hambre*.

Bread

SHARON OLDS

When my daughter makes bread, a cloud of flour
hangs in the air like pollen. She sifts and
sifts again, the salt and sugar
close as the grain of her skin. She heats the
water to body temperature
with the sausage lard, fragrant as her scalp
the day before hair-wash, and works them together on a
floured board. Her broad palms
bend the paste toward her and the heel of her hand
presses it away, until the dough
begins to snap, glossy and elastic as the
torso bending over it,
this ten-year-old girl, random specks of
yeast in her flesh beginning to heat,
her volume doubling every month now, but still
raw and hard. She slaps the dough and it
crackles under her palm, sleek and
ferocious and still leashed, like her body, no
breasts rising like bubbles of air toward the
surface of the loaf. She greases the pan, she is
shaped, glazed, and at any moment goes
into the oven, to turn to that porous
warm substance, and then under the
knife to be sliced for the having, the tasting, and the
giving of life.

MEAT & POTATOES

The only time to eat diet food is while you're waiting for the steak to cook.

—JULIA CHILD

Osso Bucco

BILLY COLLINS

I love the sound of the bone against the plate
and the fortress-like look of it
lying before me in a moat of risotto,
the meat soft as the leg of an angel
who has lived a purely airborne existence.
And best of all, the secret marrow,
the invaded privacy of the animal
prized out with a knife and swallowed down
with cold, exhilarating wine.

I am swaying now in the hour after dinner,
a citizen tilted back on his chair,
a creature with a full stomach—
something you don't hear much about in poetry,
that sanctuary of hunger and deprivation.
You know: the driving rain, the boots by the door,
small birds searching for berries in winter.

But tonight, the lion of contentment
has placed a warm, heavy paw on my chest,
and I can only close my eyes and listen
to the drums of woe throbbing in the distance
and the sound of my wife's laughter
on the telephone in the next room,
the woman who cooked the savory osso bucco,
who pointed to show the butcher the ones she wanted.
She who talks to her faraway friend

while I linger here at the table
with a hot, companionable cup of tea,
feeling like one of the friendly natives,
a reliable guide, maybe even the chief's favorite son.

Somewhere, a man is crawling up a rock hillside
on bleeding knees and palms, an Irish penitent
carrying the stone of the world in his stomach;
and elsewhere people of all nations stare
at one another across a long, empty table.

But here, the candles give off their warm glow,
the same light that Shakespeare and Izaak Walton wrote by,
the light that lit and shadowed the faces of history.
Only now it plays on the blue plates,
the crumpled napkins, the crossed knife and fork.

In a while, one of us will go up to bed
and the other one will follow.
Then we will slip below the surface of the night
into miles of water, drifting down and down
to the dark, soundless bottom
until the weight of dreams pulls us lower still,
below the shale and layered rock,
beneath the strata of hunger and pleasure,
into the broken bones of the earth itself,
into the marrow of the only place we know.

Corned Beef and Cabbage

GEORGE BILGERE

I can see her in the kitchen,
Cooking up, for the hundredth time,
A little something from her
Limited Midwestern repertoire.
Cigarette going in the ashtray,
The red wine pulsing in its glass,
A warning light meaning
Everything was simmering
Just below the steel lid
Of her smile, as she boiled
The beef into submission,
Chopped her way
Through the vegetable kingdom
With the broken-handled knife
I use tonight, feeling her
Anger rising from the dark
Chambers of the head
Of cabbage I slice through,
Missing her, wanting
To chew things over
With my mother again.

Pot Roast

MARK STRAND

I gaze upon the roast,
that is sliced and laid out
on my plate,
and over it
I spoon the juices
of carrot and onion.
And for once I do not regret
the passage of time.

I sit by a window
that looks
on a soot-stained brick of buildings
and do not care that I see
no living thing—not a bird,
not a branch in bloom,
not a soul moving
in the rooms
behind the dark panes.
These days when there is little
to love or to praise
one could do worse
than yield
to the power of food.
So I bend

to inhale
the steam that rises

from my plate, and I think
of the first time
I tasted a roast
like this.
It was years ago
in Seabright,
Nova Scotia;
my mother leaned
over my dish and filled it
and when I finished
filled it again.
I remember the gravy,
its odor of garlic and celery,
and sopping it up
with pieces of bread.

And now
I taste it again.
The meat of memory.
The meat of no change.
I raise my fork
and I eat.

Potato

RICHARD WILBUR

for André du Bouchet

An underground grower, blind and a common brown;
Got a misshapen look, it's nudged where it could;
Simple as soil yet crowded as earth with all.

Cut open raw, it looses a cool clean stench,
Mineral acid seeping from pores of prest meal;
It is like breaching a strangely refreshing tomb:

Therein the taste of first stones, the hands of dead slaves,
Waters men drank in the earliest frightful woods,
Flint chips, and peat, and the cinders of buried camps.

Scrubbed under faucet water the planet skin
Polishes yellow, but tears to the plain insides;
Parching, the white's blue-hearted like hungry hands.

All of the cold dark kitchens, and war-frozen gray
Evening at window; I remember so many
Peeling potatoes quietly into chipt pails.

"It was potatoes saved us, they kept us alive."
Then they had something to say akin to praise
For the mean earth-apples, too common to cherish or steal.

Times being hard, the Sikh and the Senegalese,
Hobo and Okie, the body of Jesus the Jew,
Vestigial virtues, are eaten; we shall survive.

What has not lost its savor shall hold us up,
And we are praising what saves us, what fills the need.
(Soon there'll be packets again, with Algerian fruits.)

Oh, it will not bear polish, the ancient potato,
Needn't be nourished by Caesars, will blow anywhere
Hidden by nature, counted-on, stubborn and blind.

You may have noticed the bush that it pushes to air,
Comical-delicate, sometimes with second-rate flowers
Awkward and milky and beautiful only to hunger.

Potato

JANE KENYON

In haste one evening while making dinner
I threw away a potato that was spoiled
on one end. The rest would have been

redeemable. In the yellow garbage pail
it became the consort of coffee grounds,
banana skins, carrot peelings.
I pitched it onto the compost
where steaming scraps and leaves
return, like bodies over time, to earth.

When I flipped the fetid layers with a hay
fork to air the pile, the potato turned up
unfailingly, as if to revile me—

looking plumper, firmer, resurrected
instead of disassembling. It seemed to grow
until I might have made shepherd's pie
for a whole hamlet, people who pass the day
dropping trees, pumping gas, pinning
hand-me-down clothes on the line.

Banking Potatoes

YUSEF KOMUNYAKAA

Daddy would drop purple-veined vines
Along rows of dark loam
& I'd march behind him
Like a peg-legged soldier,
Pushing down the stick
With a V cut into its tip.

Three weeks before the first frost
I'd follow his horse-drawn plow
That opened up the soil & left
Sweet potatoes sticky with sap,
Like flesh-colored stones along a riverbed
Or diminished souls beside a mass grave.

They lay all day under the sun's
Invisible weight, & by twilight
We'd bury them under pine needles
& then shovel in two feet of dirt.
Nighthawks scalloped the sweaty air,
Their wings spread wide

As plowshares. But soon the wind
Knocked on doors & windows
Like a frightened stranger,
& by mid-winter we had tunneled
Back into the tomb of straw,
Unable to divide love from hunger.

The Digging

RENNIE MCQUILKIN

It's that time of year,
the hedgerows hung with bittersweet.
Potato time.

How early the freeze, I'd say
if we were speaking. We're not.
We turn our spading forks against

the earth. It's stiff,
the Reds and Idahos hard as stone,
a total loss.

Once it was us against the beetles,
blight, whatever was not potato.
How they flowered, rows and rows

in white. Now look.
We give it one last try, and there
far down in softer soil,

a seam of them still perfect.
One after another
we hold them up to the dying day,

kneel down to sift for more.
In the dark of the earth, I come upon
your hand, you mine.

Potatoes

LINDA HOGAN

This is the month of warm days
and a spirit of ice
that breathes in the dark,
the month we dig potatoes
small as a child's fist.
Under soil, light skins
and lifeline to leaves and sun.

It is the way this daughter stands beside me
in close faith that I am warm
that makes me remember
so many years of the same work
preparing for quiet winter,
old women bent with children
in dusty fields.

All summer the potatoes have grown
in silence,
gentle,
moving stones away.

And my daughter has changed this way.
So many things to say to her
but our worlds are not the same.
I am the leaves, above ground in the sun
and she is small, dark,
clinging to buried roots,
holding tight to leaves.

In one day of digging the earth
there is communion
of things we remember
and forget.
We taste starch
turn to sugar in our mouths.

from Clearances

SEAMUS HEANEY

in memoriam M.K.H., 1911–1984

When all the others were away at Mass
I was all hers as we peeled potatoes.
They broke the silence, let fall one by one
Like solder weeping off the soldering iron:
Cold comforts set between us, things to share
Gleaming in a bucket of clean water.
And again let fall. Little pleasant splashes
From each other's work would bring us to our senses.

So while the parish priest at her bedside
Went hammer and tongs at the prayers for the dying
And some were responding and some crying
I remembered her head bent towards my head,
Her breath in mine, our fluent dipping knives—
Never closer the whole rest of our lives.

OFFERINGS

Our final, definite leaving of the gardens came one cold winter day, all too appropriate to our feelings and the state of the world. A sudden moment of sunshine peopled the gardens with all the friends and others who had passed through them. Ah, there would be another garden, the same friends, possibly, or no, probably new ones, and there would be other stories to tell and to hear.
—ALICE B. TOKLAS,
The Alice B. Toklas Cookbook

Arabic Coffee

NAOMI SHIHAB NYE

It was never too strong for us:
make it blacker, Papa,
thick in the bottom,
tell again how the years will gather
in small white cups,
how luck lives in a spot of grounds.

Leaning over the stove, he let it
boil to the top, and down again.
Two times. No sugar in his pot.
And the place where men and women
break off from one another
was not present in that room.
The hundred disappointments,
fire swallowing olive-wood beads
at the warehouse, and the dreams
tucked like pocket handkerchiefs
into each day, took their places
on the table, near the half-empty
dish of corn. And none was
more important than the others,
and all were guests. When
he carried the tray into the room,
high and balanced in his hands,
it was an offering to all of them,
stay, be seated, follow the talk
wherever it goes. The coffee was

the center of the flower.
Like clothes on a line saying
You will live long enough to wear me,
a motion of faith. There is this,
and there is more.

Coffee

MATTHEW DICKMAN

The only precious thing I own, this little espresso
cup. And in it a dark roast all the way
from Honduras, Guatemala, Ethiopia
where coffee was born in the 9th century
getting goat herders high, spinning like dervishes, the white blooms
cresting out of the evergreen plant, Ethiopia
where I almost lived for a moment but
then the rebels surrounded the Capital
so I stayed home. I stayed home and drank
coffee and listened to the radio
and heard how they were getting along. I would walk
down Everett Street, near the hospital
where my older brother was bound
to his white bed like a human mast, where he was
getting his mind right and learning
not to hurt himself. I would walk by and be afraid and smell
the beans being roasted inside the garage
of an old warehouse. It smelled like burnt
toast! It was everywhere in the trees. I couldn't bear to see him.
I sometimes never knew him. Sometimes
he would call. He wanted us
to sit across from each other, some coffee between us,
sober. Coffee can taste like grapefruit
or caramel, like tobacco, strawberry,
cinnamon, the oils being pushed
out of the grounds and floating to the top of a French Press,
the expensive kind I get
in the mail, the mailman with a pound of Sumatra

under his arm, ringing my doorbell,
waking me up from a night when all I had was tea
and watched a movie about the Queen of England when Spain was
     hot
for all her castles and all their ships, carved out
of fine Spanish trees, went up in flames
while back home Spaniards were growing potatoes
and coffee was making its careful way
along a giant whip
from Africa to Europe
where cafes would become famous
and people would eventually sit with their cappuccinos, the baristas
talking about the new war, a cup of sugar
on the table, a curled piece of lemon rind. A beret
on someone's head, a scarf
around their neck. A bomb in a suitcase
left beneath a small table. Right now
I'm sitting near a hospital where psychotropics are being
carried down the hall in a pink cup,
where someone is lying there and he doesn't know who
he is. I'm listening
to the couple next to me
talk about their cars. I have no idea
how I got here. The world stops at the window
while I take my little spoon and slowly swirl the cream around the lip
of the cup. Once, I had a brother
who used to sit and drink his coffee black, smoke
his cigarettes and be quiet for a moment
before his brain turned its Armadas against him, wanting to burn down
his cities and villages, before grief
became his capital with its one loyal flag and his face,
perhaps only his beautiful left eye, shimmered on the surface of his
     Americano
like a dark star.

Offering

SHARAN STRANGE

In the dream, I am burning the rice.
I am cooking for God. I will clean
the house to please Him. So I wash the dishes,
and it begins to burn. It is for luck.
Like rice pelting newlyweds,
raining down, it is another veil,
or an offering that suggests
her first duty: to feed him.

Burning, it turns brown, the color
of my father, whom I never pleased.
Too late, I stand at his bed, calling.
He is swathed in twisted sheets,
a heavy mummy that will not
eat or cry. Will he sleep when
a tall stranger comes to murder me?
Will I die this fourth time, or the next?

When I run it is as if underwater,
slow, sluggish as the swollen grains
rising out of the briny broth to fill the pot,
evicting the steam in low shrieks
like God's breath sucked back in.
Before I slip the black husk of sleep,
I complete the task. The rice chars,
crumbles to dust, to mix with
the salty water, to begin again.

When the Burning Begins

PATRICIA SMITH

for Otis Douglas Smith, my father

The recipe for hot water cornbread is simple:
Cornmeal, hot water. Mix till sluggish,
then dollop in a sizzling skillet.
When you smell the burning begin, flip it.
When you smell the burning begin again,
dump it onto a plate. You've got to wait
for the burning and get it just right.

Before the bread cools down,
smear it with sweet salted butter
and smash it with your fingers,
crumple it up in a bowl
of collard greens or buttermilk,
forget that I'm telling you it's the first thing
I ever cooked, that my daddy was laughing
and breathing and no bullet in his head
when he taught me.

Mix it till it looks like quicksand, he'd say.
Till it moves like a slow song sounds.

We'd sit there in the kitchen, licking our fingers
and laughing at my mother,
who was probably scrubbing something with bleach,
or watching *Bonanza*,

or thinking how stupid it was to be burning
that nasty old bread in that cast iron skillet.
When I told her that I'd made my first-ever pan
of hot water cornbread, and that my daddy
had branded it glorious, she sniffed and kept
mopping the floor over and over in the same place.

So here's how you do it:

You take out a bowl, like the one
we had with blue flowers and only one crack,
you put the cornmeal in it.
Then you turn on the hot water and you let it run
while you tell the story about the boy
who kissed your cheek after school
or about how you really want to be a reporter
instead of a teacher or nurse like Mama said,
and the water keeps running while Daddy says
You will be a wonderful writer
and you will be famous someday and when
you get famous, if I wrote you a letter and
send you some money, would you write about me?

and he is laughing and breathing and no bullet
in his head. So you let the water run into this mix
till it moves like mud moves at the bottom of a river,
which is another thing Daddy said, and even though
I'd never even seen a river,
I knew exactly what he meant.
Then you turn the fire way up under the skillet,
and you pour in this mix
that moves like mud moves at the bottom of a river,
like quicksand, like slow song sounds.
That stuff pops something awful when it first hits

that blazing skillet, and sometimes Daddy and I
would dance to those angry pop sounds,
he'd let me rest my feet on top of his
while we waltzed around the kitchen
and my mother huffed and puffed
on the other side of the door. *When you are famous,*
Daddy asks me, *will you write about dancing
in the kitchen with your father?*
I say everything I write will be about you,
then you will be famous too. And we dip and swirl
and spin, but then he stops.
And sniffs the air.

The thing you have to remember
about hot water cornbread
is to wait for the burning
so you know when to flip it, and then again
so you know when it's crusty and done.
Then eat it the way we did,
with our fingers,
our feet still tingling from dancing.
But remember that sometimes the burning
takes such a long time,
and in that time,
sometimes,

poems are born.

The Onion

MARGARET GIBSON

Mornings when sky is white as dried gristle
and the air's unhealthy, coast
smothered, and you gone
                I could stay in bed
and be the woman who aches for no reason, each day
a small death of love, cold rage for dinner,
coffee and continental indifference
at dawn.
            Or dream lazily a market day—
bins of fruit and celery, poultry strung up,
loops of garlic and peppers. I'd select one
yellow onion, fist-sized, test its sleek
hardness, haggle, and settle a fair price.

Yesterday, a long day measured by shovel
and mattock, a wrestle with roots—
calm and dizzy when I bent over to loosen my shoes
at the finish—I thought
                if there were splendors,
what few there were, knowledge of them
in me like fire in flint
I would have them . . .
              and now I'd say the onion,
I'd have that, too. The work it took,
the soup it flavors, the griefs
innocently it summons.

Tomatoes

STEPHEN DOBYNS

A woman travels to Brazil for plastic
surgery and a face-lift. She is sixty
and has the usual desire to stay pretty.
Once she is healed, she takes her new face
out on the streets of Rio. A young man
with a gun wants her money. Bang, she's dead.
The body is shipped back to New York,
but in the morgue there is a mix-up. The son
is sent for. He is told that his mother
is one of these ten different women.
Each has been shot. Such is modern life.
He studies them all but can't find her.
With her new face, she has become a stranger.
Maybe it's this one, maybe it's that one.
He looks at her breasts. Which ones nursed him?
He presses their heads to his cheek.
Which ones consoled him? He even tries
climbing into their laps to see which
feels most familiar but the coroner stops him.
Well, says the coroner, which is your mother?
They all are, says the young man, let me
take them as a package. The coroner hesitates,
then agrees. Actually, it solved a lot of problems.
The young man has the ten women shipped home,
then cremates them all together. You've seen
how some people have a little urn on the mantel?
This man has a huge silver garbage can.

In the spring, he drags the garbage can
out to the garden and begins working the teeth,
the ash, the bits of bone into the soil.
Then he plants tomatoes. His mother loved tomatoes.
They grow straight from seed, so fast and big
that the young man is amazed. He takes the first
ten into the kitchen. In their roundness,
he sees his mother's breasts. In their smoothness,
he finds the consoling touch of her hands.
Mother, mother, he cries, and flings himself
on the tomatoes. Forget about the knife, the fork,
the pinch of salt. Try to imagine the filial
starvation, think of his ravenous kisses.

Ode to Gumbo

KEVIN YOUNG

For weeks I have waited
for a day without death
or doubt. Instead
the sky set afire

or the flood
filling my face.
A stubborn drain
nothing can fix.

Every day death.
Every morning death
& every night
& evening

And each hour
a kind of winter—
all weather
is unkind. Too

hot, or cold
that creeps the bones.
Father, your face
a faith

I can no longer see.
Across the street

a dying, yet
still-standing tree.

⌒

So why not
make a soup
of what's left? Why
not boil & chop

something outside
the mind—let us
welcome winter
for a few hours, even

in summer. Some
say Gumbo
starts with *filé*
or with *roux*, begins

with flour & water
making sure
not to burn. I know Gumbo
starts with sorrow—

with hands that cannot wait
but must—with stirring
& a slow boil
& things that cannot

be taught, like grace.
Done right,
Gumbo lasts for days.
Done right, it will feed

you & not let go.
Like grief
you can eat & eat
& still plenty

left. Food
of the saints,
Gumbo will outlast
even us—like pity,

you will curse it
& still hope
for the wing
of chicken bobbed

up from below.
Like God
Gumbo is hard
to get right

& I don't bother
asking for it outside
my mother's house.
Like life, there's no one

way to do it,
& a hundred ways,
from here to Sunday,
to get it dead wrong.

Save all the songs.
I know none,
even this, that will
bring a father

back to his son.
Blood is thicker
than water under
any bridge

& Gumbo thicker
than that. It was
my father's mother
who taught mine how

to stir its dark mirror—
now it is me
who wishes to plumb
its secret

depths. Black
Angel, Madonna
of the Shadows,
Hail Mary strong

& dark as dirt,
Gumbo's scent fills
this house like silence
& tells me everything

has an afterlife, given
enough time & the right
touch. You need
okra, sausage, bones

of a bird, an entire
onion cut open
& wept over, stirring
cayenne in till the end

burns the throat—
till we can amen
& pretend
such fiery

mercy is all we know.

Orchard

ROSANNA WARREN

in memoriam W.K.

Crippled by years of pruning, the apple branch
bends toward me, and I pick
the wizened, fiery fruit you offered years
ago, as you were dying.

Years, it took, for the fact
of your simply not
answering to ripen
within me. Only now

as I sit, pregnant, marooned
in tall grass, cross-hatched
by October sunlight, with the *thunk*
of apples falling, can I taste

your absence. Pale
green, acidic. A spurt
of saliva quickens the mouth.
From the lower field

float yelps and laughter
of children tussling among
hummocks. Their fathers grope
higher into the branches, hands

stretching to grasp
that flecked, streaked
russets and McIntosh. Those men
are woven into a basketwork of boughs

and I am heavy on the ground below
surrounded
by bruised fruit and a fermenting
glow that rises

as apple haze from the weeds.
You had no children.
But you gave
me a painting of apples

shrivelled and burning,
which I remember now
and again, so that I may
learn, as you did, how

passionately to die. In
time, in time. My child
stirring within me weighs me down.
You have come

to meet us through
the braided seasons, and I see
how, rusting and golden, already
we are following you.

Maple Syrup

DONALD HALL

August, goldenrod blowing. We walk
into the graveyard, to find
my grandfather's grave. Ten years ago
I came here last, bringing
marigolds from the round garden
outside the kitchen.
I didn't know you then.
                      We walk
among carved names that go with photographs
on top of the piano at the farm:
Keneston, Wells, Fowler, Batchelder, Buck.
We pause at the new grave
of Grace Fenton, my grandfather's
sister. Last summer
we called on her at the nursing home,
eighty-seven, and nodding
in a blue housedress. We cannot find
my grandfather's grave
                         Back at the house
where no one lives, we potter
and explore the back chamber
where everything comes to rest: spinning wheels,
pretty boxes, quilts,
bottles, books, albums of postcards.
Then with a flashlight we descend
frail steps to the root cellar—black,
cobwebby, huge,

with dirt floors and fieldstone walls,
and above the walls, holding the hewn
sills of the house, enormous
granite foundation stones.
Past the empty bins
for squash, apples, carrots, and potatoes,
we discover the shelves for canning, a few
pale pints
of tomato left, and—what
is this?—syrup, maple syrup
in a quart jar, syrup
my grandfather made twenty-five
years ago
for the last time.
                              I remember
coming to the farm in March
in sugaring time, as a small boy.
He carried the pails of sap, sixteen-quart
buckets, dangling from each end
of a wooden yoke
that lay across his shoulders, and emptied them
into a vat in the saphouse
where fire burned day and night
for a week.
                              Now the saphouse
tilts, nearly to the ground,
like someone exhausted
to the point of death, and next winter
when snow piles three feet thick
on the roofs of the cold farm,
the saphouse will shudder and slide
with the snow to the ground.
                              Today
we take my grandfather's last

quart of syrup
upstairs, holding it gingerly,
and we wash off twenty-five years
of dirt, and we pull
and pry the lid up, cutting the stiff,
dried rubber gasket, and dip our fingers
in, you and I both, and taste
the sweetness, you for the first time,
the sweetness preserved, of a dead man
in the kitchen he left
when his body slid
like anyone's into the ground.

Lasting

W. D. SNODGRASS

"Fish oils," my doctor snorted, "and oily fish
are actually good for you. What's actually wrong
for anyone your age are all those dishes
with thick sauce that we all pined for so long
as we were young and poor. Now we can afford
to order such things, just not to digest them;
we find what bills we've run up in the stored
plaque and fat cells of our next stress test."

My own last test scored in the top 10 percent
of males in my age bracket. Which defies
all consequences or justice—I've spent
years shackled to my desk, saved from all exercise.
My dentist, next: "Your teeth seem quite good
for someone your age, better than we'd expect
with so few checkups or cleanings. Teeth should
repay you with more grief for such neglect"—

echoing how my mother always nagged,
"Brush a full 100 strokes," and would jam
cod liver oil down our throats till we'd go gagging
off to flu-filled classrooms, crammed
with vegetables and vitamins. By now,
I've outlasted both parents whose plain food
and firm ordinance must have endowed
this heart's tough muscle—weak still in gratitude.

Spell to Be Said After Illness

JANE HIRSHFIELD

Crabapple holding in arms
what almost has
vanished,
selvage and leaf-lavish open.

Pumpkin seed in the hand,
lick the salt after.
What remains, after.
Bowl fill with woodpecker's shavings of cedar.

Door of the beak, release attic.
Voice remain fragrant.
Love hold the lungs again open.

By the bed, here.
By silence and whiteness,
by staying.
Carved scent of orange-oil, open.

By rise of the woodpecker's question,
of crabapple fruiting,
clasp now this room that is given.

Open with flood what is given,
once again fragrant and here.

Eating the Cookies

JANE KENYON

The cousin from Maine, knowing
about her diverticulitis, let out the nuts,
so the cookies weren't entirely to my taste,
but they were good enough; yes, good enough.

Each time I emptied a drawer or shelf
I permitted myself to eat one.
I cleared the closet of silk caftans
that slipped easily from clattering hangers,
and from the bureau I took her nightgowns
and sweaters, financial documents
neatly cinctured in long gray envelopes,
and the hairnets and peppermints she'd tucked among
Lucite frames abounding with great grandchildren,
solemn in their Christmas finery.

Finally the drawers were empty,
the bags full, and the largest cookie,
which I had saved for last, lay
solitary in the tin with a nimbus
of crumbs around it. There would be no more
parcels from Portland. I took it up
and sniffed it, and before eating it,
pressed it against my forehead, because
it seemed like the next thing to do.

The Soup

CHARLES SIMIC

Together in the pot
With our lives
Chopped like onions.

Let it rain, let it snow.
Dead people's wedding pictures
Make a hearty soup.

The soup of strays
Roaming the world
In search of their master.

The soup of orphans
Wiping their red noses
On the black armband on their sleeves.

The soup loved by flies.

On what shall we cook it?

On the mustache of Joseph Stalin.
The fires of Treblinka.
The fires of Hiroshima.
The head of the one about to be shot.
The head swarming with memories.

Let's cook it until we see in its steam
Our sweethearts' white bodies.
They are huge, they are voluptuous,
They are offering their breasts to us
As if we were suckling infants.

What do you think it will taste like?

Like spit on a pair of dice.
Like prison barbed wire.
Like white panties of Veronica Lake.
Like her toes painted red.
Like tallow on death's wheelbarrow.

At the end of an evil century,
We arouse the devil's curiosity
By spooning the soup of angels
Into our toothless mouths.

What shall we eat it with?

With an old shoe left in the rain.
With two eyes quarreling in the same head.
With a bent and rusty nail
And a trembling hand.

We'll sit slurping
With our hats on:
A soup like knives being sharpened.
A thick slaughterhouse soup.

And this is what we'll have on the side:

The bread of remembrance, a black bread.
Blood sausages of yes and no.
Scallions grown on our mothers' graves.
Black olives from our fathers' eyes.

The immigrant in the middle of the Atlantic,
Pissing in the sea with a sense of eternity.
The wine of that clear night,
A dark wine sparkling with stars.

Christmas in Chinatown

AUGUST KLEINZAHLER

They're off doing what they do
and it is pleasant to be here without them
taking up so much room.
They are safely among their own,
in front of their piles of meat, arguing
about cars and their generals,
and, of course, with the TV going all the while.

One reads that the digestive wind passed by cattle
is many times more destructive to the atmosphere
than all of the aerosol cans combined.
How does one measure such a thing?
The world has been coming to an end
for 5,000 years. If not tomorrow,
surely, one day very soon.

Wintering

SYLVIA PLATH

This is the easy time, there is nothing doing.
I have whirled the midwife's extractor,
I have my honey,
Six jars of it,
Six cat's eyes in the wine cellar,

Wintering in a dark without window
At the heart of the house
Next to the last tenant's rancid jam
And the bottles of empty glitters——
Sir So-and-so's gin.

This is the room I have never been in.
This is the room I could never breathe in.
The black bunched in there like a bat,
No light
But the torch and its faint

Chinese yellow on appalling objects——
Black asininity. Decay.
Possession.
It is they who own me.
Neither cruel nor indifferent,

Only ignorant.
This is the time of hanging on for the bees—the bees
So slow I hardly know them,

Filing like soldiers
To the syrup tin

To make up for the honey I've taken.
Tate and Lyle keeps them going,
The refined snow.
It is Tate and Lyle they live on, instead of flowers.
They take it. The cold sets in.

Now they ball in a mass,
Black
Mind against all that white.
The smile of the snow is white.
It spreads itself out, a mile-long body of Meissen,

Into which, on warm days,
They can only carry their dead.
The bees are all women,
Maids and the long royal lady.
They have got rid of the men,

The blunt, clumsy stumblers, the boors.
Winter is for women——
The woman, still at her knitting,
At the cradle of Spanish walnut,
Her body a bulb in the cold and too dumb to think.

Will the hive survive, will the gladiolas
Succeed in banking their fires
To enter another year?
What will they taste of, the Christmas roses?
The bees are flying. They taste the spring.

III.
Spring Rain

Nothing is so beautiful as spring.
— GERARD MANLEY HOPKINS

PIG OUT

*Now what has all this to do with anything, well
anything always has something to do with something and
nothing is more interesting than that something that you eat.*
—GERTRUDE STEIN
American Food and American Houses

Ode to Pork

KEVIN YOUNG

I wouldn't be here
without you. Without you
I'd be umpteen
pounds lighter & a lot
less alive. You stuck
round my ribs even
when I treated you like a dog
dirty, I dare not eat.
I know you're the blues
because loving you
may kill me—but still you
rock me down slow
as hamhocks on the stove.
Anyway you come
fried, cued, burnt
to within one inch
of your life I love. Babe,
I revere your every
nickname—bacon, chitlin,
crackling, sin.
Some call you murder,
shame's step-sister—
then dress you up
& declare you white
& healthy, but you always
come back, sauced, to me.
Adam himself gave up

a rib to see yours
piled pink beside him.
Your heaven is the only one
worth wanting—
you keep me all night
cursing your four-
letter name, the next
begging for you again.

Circe

CAROL ANN DUFFY

I'm fond, nereids and nymphs, unlike some, of the pig,
Of the tusker, the snout, the boar and the swine.
One way or another, all pigs have been mine—
Under my thumb, the bristling, salty skin of their backs,
In my nostrils here, their yobby, porky colognes.
I'm familiar with hogs and runts, their percussion of oinks
At dusk, at the creaky gate of the sty,
Tasting the sweaty, spicy air, the moon
Like a lemon popped in the mouth of the sky.
But I want to begin with a recipe from abroad

which uses the cheek—and the tongue in cheek
at that. Lay two pig's cheeks, with the tongue,
in a dish, and strew it well over with salt
and cloves. Remember the skills of the tongue—
to lick, to lap, to loosen, lubricate, to lie
in the soft pouch of the face—and how each pig's face
was uniquely itself, as many handsome as plain,
the cowardly face, the brave, the comical, noble,
sly or wise, the cruel, the kind, but all of them,
nymphs, with those piggy eyes. Season with mace.

Bacon & Eggs

HOWARD NEMEROV

The chicken contributes,
But the pig gives his all.

Song to Bacon

ROY BLOUNT JR.

Consumer groups have gone and taken
Some of the savor out of bacon.
Protein-per-penny in bacon, they say,
Equals needles-per-square-inch of hay.
Well, I know, after cooking all
That's left to eat is mighty small
      (You also get a lot of lossage
      In life, romance, and country sausage),
And I will vote for making it cheaper,
Wider, longer, leaner, deeper,
But let's not throw the baby, please,
Out with the (visual rhyme here) grease.
There's nothing crumbles like bacon still,
And I don't think there ever will
Be anything, whate'er you use
For meat, that chews like bacon chews.
And also: I wish these groups would tell
Me whether they counted in the smell.
The smell of it cooking's worth $2.10 a pound.
And how bout the *sound*?

1-800-Hot-Ribs

CATHERINE BOWMAN

My brother sent me ribs for my birthday.
He sent me two six-pound, heavily scented,
slow-smoked slabs, Federal Express,
in a customized cardboard box, no bigger
than a baby coffin or a bulrush ark.

Swaddled tight in sheaves of foam and dry ice,
those ribs rested in the hold of some jetliner
and were carried high, over the Yellowhammer State
and the Magnolia State and the Brown Thrasher State,
over Kentucky coffeetrees and Sitka spruce

and live oak and wild oak and lowland plains
and deep-water harbors, over catfish farms
and single-crib barns and Holiness sects
and strip malls and mill towns and lumber
towns and coal camps and chemical plants,

to my table on this island on a cold night
with no moon where I eat those ribs and am made
full from what must have been a young animal,
small-boned and tender, having just
the right ratio of meat to fat.

Tonight outside, men and women enrobed
in blankets fare forth from shipping crates.
A bloodhound lunges against its choke

to sniff the corpse of a big rat and heaps
of drippings and grounds that steam

outside the diner as an ashen woman deep
in a doorway presses a finger to her lips.
A matted teddy bear impaled on a spike
looms over a vacant lot where a line of men
wreathe in fellowship around a blazing garbage can.

Tonight in a dream they gather
all night to labor over the unadorned
beds they have dug into the ground and filled
with the hardwood coals that glow like remote stars.
Their faces molten and ignited in the damp,

they know to turn the meat infrequently,
they know to keep the flame slow and the fire
cool. From a vat of spirits subacid and brackish,
they know to baste only occasionally. So that
by sunrise vapor will continue to collect, as usual,

forming, as it should, three types of clouds,
that the rainfall from the clouds, it is certain,
will not exceed the capacity of the river,
that the river will still flow, as always,
sweet brother, on course.

The Gospel of Barbecue

HONORÉE JEFFERS

for Alvester James

Long after it was
necessary, Uncle
Vess ate the leavings
off the hog, doused
them with vinegar sauce.
He ate chewy abominations.
Then came high pressure.
Then came the little pills.
Then came the doctor
who stole Vess's second
sight, the predication
of pig's blood every
fourth Sunday.
Then came the stillness
of barn earth, no more
trembling at his step.
Then came the end
of the rib, but before
his eyes clouded,
Uncle Vess wrote
down the gospel
of barbecue.

Chapter one:
Somebody got to die

with something at some
time or another.

Chapter two:
Don't ever trust
white folk to cook
your meat until
it's done to the bone.

Chapter three:
December is the best
time for hog killing.
The meat won't
spoil as quick.
Screams and blood
freeze over before
they hit the air.

Chapter four, Verse one:
Great Grandma Mandy
used to say food
you was whipped
for tasted the best.

Chapter four, Verse two:
Old Master knew to lock
the ham bacon chops
away quick or the slaves
would rob him blind.
He knew a padlock
to the smokehouse
was best to prevent
stealing, but even the
sorriest of slaves would

risk a beating for a full
belly. So Christmas time
he give his nasty
leftovers to the well
behaved. The head ears
snout tail fatback
chitlins feet ribs balls.
He thought gratitude
made a good seasoning.

Chapter five:
Unclean means dirty
means filthy means
underwear worn too
long in summertime heat.
Perfectly good food
can't be no sin.
Maybe the little
bit of meat on ribs
makes for lean eating.
Maybe the pink flesh
is tasteless until you add
onions garlic black
pepper tomatoes
soured apple cider
but survival ain't never been
no crime against nature
or Maker. See, stay alive
in the meantime, laugh
a little harder. Go on
and gnaw that bone clean.

Sooey Generous

WILLIAM MATTHEWS

Saint Anthony, patron of sausage makers,
guide my pen and unkink my tongue. Of swine
I sing, and of those who tend and slaughter them,
of slops and wallows and fodder, of piglets
doddering on their stilty legs, and sows
splayed to offer burgeoned teats to sucklers,
and the four to five tons of manure
a pig (that ambling buffet) reinvests
in the soil each year; of truffle dowsers
and crunchers of chestnuts and acorns I sing.

In medieval Naples, each household
kept a pig on a twenty-four-foot tether,
rope enough that the hooved Hoover could
scour the domain, whereas in Rome
pigs foraged the streets haunted today by
rat-thin cats, tendons with fur. In Paris
in those years the *langueyers*, the "tonguers,"
or meat inspectors, lifted a pig's tongue
to look for white ulcers, since the comely
pig in spoiled condition could poison

a family. Indeed the Buddha died
from eating spoiled pork, vegetarians
I know like to insist, raising the stakes
from wrong to fatal, gleefully. Perhaps
you've read the bumper sticker too: *A Heart*

Attack Is God's Revenge for Eating His
Little Friends. Two major religions
prohibit eating pork. Both creeds were forged
in deserts, and the site-specific pig,
who detests dry mud, has never mixed well

with nomads or vice versa. Since a pig
eats everything, just as the cuisines that
sanctify the pig discard no fragment
of it, it makes sense to eat it whole hog
or shun it altogether, since to eat
or not to eat is sacral, if there's a choice
in the matter. To fast is not to starve.
The thirteen ravenous, sea-queasy pigs
Hernando de Soto loosed near Tampa
in 1542 ate whatever

they liked. How glad they must have been to hoove
some soil after skidding in the slick hold
week after dark week: a pig without sun
on its sullied back grows skittish and glum.
Pigs and pioneers would build America.
Cincinnati was called Porkopolis
in the 1830s; the hogs arrived,
as the hunger for them had, by river,
from which a short forced march led to slaughter.
A new country travels on its belly,

and manufacture starts in the barnyard:
hide for leather and stomach for pepsin.
In France, a farm family calls its pig
"Monsieur." According to a CIA
tally early in 1978,
the Chinese kept 280 million

of the world's 400 million pigs;
perhaps all of them were called "The Chairman."
Emmaeus, swineherd to Odysseus,
guarded 600 sows and their litters

(the males slept outside), and no doubt each sow
and piglet had its own name in that rich
matriarchal mire. And I like to think
that in that mild hospice future pork roasts
fattened toward oblivion with all
the love and dignity that husbandry
has given up to be an industry,
and that the meat of Emmaeus's coddled
porkers tasted a little sweeter for
the graces of affection and a name.

Remembering Kitchens

THYLIAS MOSS

In the kitchen we compensate for missiles
in the world by fluting edges of crust
to bake rugged, primping rosettes and peaks
on cakes that are round tables with white
butter cloths swirled on, portable
Communion altars.

On the Sundays, ham toasted itself
with lipid melts, the honey veneer
waxed pork conceit to unnameable luster
and humps of rump poked
through the center of pineapple slices
so as to form tonsured clerical heads,
the Sundays being exceptional.

The waiting for the bread
helped us learn, when it arrived steaming
like kicked-up chariot dust then died down
quickly the staid attitude of its brown dress,
the lovely practical.
In the center of the table
we let it loaf. When that was through
we sliced it into a file to rival the keeping
of the Judgment notes. So we kept our own,
a second set, and judged the judges, toasting
with cranberry water in Libbey glasses
that came from deep in the Duz. All this
in moon's skim light.

Somehow the heat of the stove,
flames shooting up tall and blue, good looking
in the uniform, had me pulling down the door,
the seat of the Tappan's pants, having the heat push
against me, melting off my pancake makeup, nearly
a chrysalis moment, my face registering then
at least four hundred degrees, and rising
in knowledge, the heat rising too, touching
off the sensors for the absolute mantra
of the ringing, the heat sizzling through cornices
and shingles, until the house is a warm alternative
to heavenly and hellish extremes,
and I remove Mama's sweet potato pie, one made
—as are her best—in her sleep when she can't
interfere, when she's dreaming at the countertop
that turns silk beside her elegant leaning, I slice it
and put the whipped cream on quick, while the pie
is hot so the peaks of cream will froth; these
are the Sundays my family suckles grace.

Song to Barbecue Sauce

ROY BLOUNT JR.

Hot and sweet and red and greasy,
I could eat a gallon easy:
Barbecue sauce!
Lay it on, hoss.

Nothing is dross
Under barbecue sauce.

Brush it on chicken, slosh it on pork,
Eat it with fingers, not with a fork.
I could eat barbecued turtle or squash—
I could eat tar paper cooked and awash
In barbecue sauce.

I'd eat Spanish moss
With barbecue sauce.

Hear this from Evelyn Billiken Husky,
Formerly Evelyn B. of Sandusky:
"Ever since locating down in the South,
I have had barbecue sauce on my mouth."

Nothing can gloss
Over barbecue sauce.

United States of Barbecue

JAKE ADAM YORK

Mud Creek, Dreamland, Twixt-n-Tween,
the cue-joints rise through smoke
and glow like roadhouses on Heaven's way.
Or so the local gospels raise them,
each tongue ready to map the ramshackle
of shacks and houses, secret windows
and business-sector hip in some new
geography of truth. If the meek shall,
then a rib-mobile may shame the fixed pit
in a reading from the book of skill,
the grill-less one cook himself to legend
rib by rib. The great chain's links
are live and hermetic as bone
and where cue burns hotter than politics,
every mouth's the forge of change,
all scholars temporary and self-proclaimed.
One says he half-sublimes each time he eats
a rib and expects to go in a puff of smoke
when he finds the perfect pig:
he wanders like a ghost, his eyes
trying everything, a genuine R & D,
and once a day he proclaims the latest find,
a homegrown Moses canting
a vernacular talmud changeable as wind.
A word could crumple him, some backyard
master slapping mustard on a country rib
to turn the state of things entire.

So every word reverberates and mystery's
sown again. Rib or rump, dry-rub or ketchup,
the eternal terms turn and barbecue's rooted
or pulled anew. Theories proliferate
like flies after rain, but that's the usual business
where Georgia and the Carolinas river in,
the wind spirits Mississippi or Caríb,
and piedmont's melted to the uplands
in open hearths and coke ovens, stitched tight
in cotton fields, and a kudzu vine's
the proper compass. Beef or pork,
catfish, quail or armadillo,
we've tried it all, loved it with brushes,
kiss of vinegar, tongue of flame,
so whatever it may not be,
we've covered all it is. Vegetarian
exception opens eggplant, means tofu's
the next horizon, purity an envelope
that's always opening. So summer afternoons
and Saturdays when the fires go up,
smoke rises to a signal and shapes
the single common word,
hand-made silence talking on every tongue.

DOWN THE HATCH

*Heaven and earth have always loved wine,
so how could loving wine shame heaven?*

—LI PO

We have a huge barrel of wine . . .

RUMI

We have a huge barrel of wine, but no cups.
That's fine with us. Every morning
we glow and in the evening we glow again.

They say there's no future for us. They're right.
Which is fine with us.

Translated by Coleman Banks

Waiting for Wine That Doesn't Come

LI PO

Jade winejars tied in blue silk. . . .
What's taking that wineseller so long?

Mountain flowers smiling, taunting me,
it's the perfect time to sip some wine,

ladle it out beneath my east window
at dusk, wandering orioles back again.

Spring breezes and their drunken guest:
today, we were meant for each other.

Translated by David Hinton

Something Said, Waking
Drunk on a Spring Day

LI PO

It's like boundless dream here in this
world, nothing anywhere to trouble us.

I have, therefore, been drunk all day,
a shambles of sleep on the front porch.

Coming to, I look into the courtyard.
There's a bird among blossoms calling,

and when I ask what season this is,
an oriole's voice drifts on spring winds.

Overcome, verging on sorrow and lament,
I pour another drink. Soon, awaiting

the bright moon, I'm chanting a song.
And now it's over, I've forgotten why.

Translated by David Hinton

Jet

TONY HOAGLAND

Sometimes I wish I were still out
on the back porch, drinking jet fuel
with the boys, getting louder and louder
as the empty cans drop out of our paws
like booster rockets falling back to Earth

and we soar up into the summer stars.
Summer. The big sky river rushes overhead,
bearing asteroids and mist, blind fish
and old space suits with skeletons inside.
On Earth, men celebrate their hairiness,

and it is good, a way of letting life
out of the box, uncapping the bottle
to let the effervescence gush
through the narrow, usually constricted neck.

And now the crickets plug in their appliances
in unison, and then the fireflies flash
dots and dashes in the grass, like punctuation
for the labyrinthine, untrue tales of sex
someone is telling in the dark, though

no one really hears. We gaze into the night
as if remembering the bright unbroken planet
we once came from,
to which we will never

be permitted to return.
We are amazed how hurt we are.
We would give anything for what we have.

Fun

WYN COOPER

"All I want is to have a little fun
Before I die," says the man next to me
Out of nowhere, apropos of nothing. He says
His name's William but I'm sure he's Bill
Or Billy, Mac or Buddy; he's plain ugly to me,
And I wonder if he's ever had fun in his life.

We are drinking beer at noon on Tuesday,
In a bar that faces a giant car wash.
The good people of the world are washing their cars
On their lunch hours, hosing and scrubbing
As best they can in skirts and suits.
They drive their shiny Datsuns and Buicks
Back to the phone company, the record store,
The genetic engineering lab, but not a single one
Appears to be having fun like Billy and me.

I like a good beer buzz early in the day,
And Billy likes to peel the labels
From his bottles of Bud and shred them on the bar.
Then he lights every match in an oversized pack,
Letting each one burn down to his thick fingers
Before blowing and cursing them out.

A happy couple enters the bar, dangerously close
To one another, like this is a motel,
But they clean up their act when we give them

A Look. One quick beer and they're out,
Down the road and in the next state
For all I care, smiling like idiots.
We cover sports and politics and once,
When Billy burns his thumb and lets out a yelp,
The bartender looks up from his want-ads.

Otherwise the bar is ours, and the day and the night
And the car wash too, the matches and the Buds
And the clean and dirty cars, the sun and the moon
And every motel on this highway. It's ours, you hear?
And we've got plans, so relax and let us in—
All we want is to have a little fun.

Another Beer

WILLIAM MATTHEWS

The first one was for the clock
and its one song
which is the song's name.

Then a beer for the scars in the table,
all healed in the shape of initials.

Then a beer for the thirst
and its one song we keep forgetting.

And a beer for the hands
we are keeping to ourselves.
The body's dogs, they lie
by the ashtray and thump
suddenly in their sleep.

And a beer for our reticence,
the true tongue, the one song,
the fire made of air.

Then a beer for the juke box.
I wish it had the recording
of a Marcel Marceau mime performance:
28 minutes of silence,
2 of applause.

And a beer for the phone booth.
In this confessional you can sit.
You sing it your one song.

And let's have a beer for whoever goes home
and sprawls, like the remaining sock,
in the drawer of his bed and repeats
the funny joke and pulls it
shut and sleeps.

And a beer for anyone
who can't tell the difference between
death and a good cry
with its one song.
None of us will rest enough.

The last beer is always for the road.
The road is what the car drinks
traveling on its tongue of light
all the way home.

Beer for Breakfast

FRANK O'HARA

It's the month of May in my heart as the song
says and everything's perfect: a little too chilly
for April and the chestnut trees are refusing to bloom
as they should refuse if they don't want to, sky
clear and blue with a lot of side-paddle steamers
pushing through to Stockholm where the canals're true-blue

in my spacious quarters on the rue de l'Université
I give a cocktail in the bathroom, everyone gets wet
it's very beachy; and I clear my head staring at the sign
LOI DU 29 JUILLET 1881
                    so capitalizing on a few memories
from childhood by forgetting them, I'm happy as a finger
of Vermouth being poured over a slice of veal, it's
the new reality in the city of Balzac! praying to be let
into the cinema and become and influence, carried through
streets on the shoulders of Messrs Chabrol and Truffaut
towards Nice
             or do you think that the Golden Lion
would taste pleasanter (not with vermouth, lion!)?
no, but San Francisco, maybe, and abalone

                                    there is
nothing in the world I wouldn't do foryouforyou (zip!)
and I go off to meet Mario and Marc at the Flore

A Drinking Song

W. B. YEATS

Wine comes in at the mouth
And love comes in at the eye;
That's all we shall know for truth
Before we grow old and die.
I lift the glass to my mouth,
I look at you, and I sigh.

Two Drinking Songs

PAUL ZIMMER

ZIMMER REPUDIATES BEER

It is an idiot's way to die,
Therefore when you next see me
I will look like a cactus needle
Sans body, liquid, and weight,
But keen enough to make you pay.
No more will I raise the glass
And swallow till I see the froth.
I swear by the Muse that I will
Cease this slaughtering of brain cells
And no longer build this stomach
Brick by brick and glass by glass
Until the lights grow dim.
Though in summer it cools me
And in winter it warms my soul,
I herewith deny this perfection.

ZIMMER RESISTING TEMPERANCE

Some people view life as food served
By a psychopath. They do not trust it.
But Zimmer expects always to be happy.
Puzzled by melancholy, he pours a reward
And loves this world relentlessly.

Years ago he saw a snake suck light from
A frog's eyes. Now with his drink in hand,
He swallows and feels his own brain implode,
The vessels in his nose begin to glow.
Each day he plans to end up squatting like
Mahatma Gandhi with a glass of unsweetened tea.
He wishes he looked like a Rouault Christ.
But who says Zimmer should not compensate himself?
Though worn out at both ends,
He regards his happy middle,
His gilded eyes in the mirror.

Someday he may fall face down
In the puke of his own buoyancy,
But while the world and his body
Are breaking down,
Zimmer will hold his glass up.

Two Hangovers

JAMES WRIGHT

NUMBER ONE

I slouch in bed.
Beyond the streaked trees of my window,
All groves are bare.
Locusts and poplars change to unmarried women
Sorting slate from anthracite
Between railroad ties:
The yellow-bearded winter of the depression
Is still alive somewhere, an old man
Counting his collection of bottle caps
In a tarpaper shack under the cold trees
Of my grave.

I still feel half drunk,
And all those old women beyond my window
Are hunching toward the graveyard.

Drunk, mumbling Hungarian,
The sun staggers in,
And his big stupid face pitches
Into the stove.
For two hours I have been dreaming
Of green butterflies searching for diamonds
In coal seams;
And children chasing each other for a game
Through the hills of fresh graves.

But the sun has come home drunk from the sea,
And a sparrow outside
Sings of the Hanna Coal Co. and the dead moon.
The filaments of cold light bulbs tremble
In music like delicate birds.
Ah, turn it off.

NUMBER TWO:
I TRY TO WAKEN AND GREET THE WORLD ONCE AGAIN

In a pine tree,
A few yards away from my window sill,
A brilliant blue jay is springing up and down, up and down,
On a branch.
I laugh, as I see him abandon himself
To entire delight, for he knows as well as I do
That the entire branch will not break.

Frying Trout While Drunk

LYNN EMANUEL

Mother is drinking to forget a man
Who could fill the woods with invitations:
Come with me he whispered and she went
In his Nash Rambler, its dash
Where her knees turned green
In the radium dials of the '50s.
When I drink it is always 1953,
Bacon wilting in the pan on Cook Street
And mother, wrist deep in red water,
Laying a trail from the sink
To a glass of gin and back.
She is a beautiful, unlucky woman
In love with a man of lechery so solid
You could build a table on it
And when you did the blues would come to visit.
I remember all of us awkwardly at dinner,
The dark slung across the porch,
And then mother's dress falling to the floor,
Buttons ticking like seeds spit on a plate.
When I drink I am too much like her—
The knife in one hand and in the other
The trout with a belly white as my wrist.
I have loved you all my life
She told him and it was true
In the same way that all her life
She drank, dedicated to the act itself,

She stood at this stove
And with the care of the very drunk
Handed him the plate.

Party Politics

PHILIP LARKIN

I never remember holding a full drink.
My first look shows the level half-way down.
What next? Ration the rest, and try to think
Of higher things, until mine host comes round?

Some people say, best show an empty glass:
Someone will fill it. Well, I've tried that too.
You may get drunk, or dry half-hours may pass.
It seems to turn on where you are. Or who.

Be Drunk

CHARLES BAUDELAIRE

You have to be always drunk. That's all there is to it—it's the only way.
So as not to feel the horrible burden of time that breaks your back
and bends you to the earth, you have to be continually drunk.

But on what? Wine, poetry or virtue, as you wish. But be drunk.

And if sometimes, on the steps of a palace or the green grass of
a ditch, in the mournful solitude of your room, you wake again,
drunkenness already diminishing or gone, ask the wind, the wave,
the star, the bird, the clock, everything that is flying, everything that
is groaning, everything that is rolling, everything that is singing,
everything that is speaking . . . ask what time it is and wind, wave,
star, bird, clock will answer you: "It is time to be drunk! So as not to
be the martyred slaves of time, be drunk, be continually drunk! On
wine, on poetry or on virtue as you wish."

Translated by Louis Simpson

from Muse & Drudge

HARRYETTE MULLEN

wine's wicked wine's divine
pickled drunk down to the rind
depression ham ain't got no bone
watermelons rampant emblazoned

island named Dawta
Gullah backwater
she swim she fish
here it be fresh

cassava yucca taro dasheen
spicy yam okra vinegary greens
guava salt cod catfish ackee
fatmeat's greasy that's too easy

not to be outdone she put
the big pot in the little pot
when you get food this good
you know the cook stuck her foot in it

Litany

BILLY COLLINS

You are the bread and the knife,
The crystal goblet and the wine.
—JACQUES CRICKILLON

You are the bread and the knife,
the crystal goblet and the wine.
You are the dew on the morning grass,
and the burning wheel of the sun.
You are the white apron of the baker
and the marsh birds suddenly in flight.

However, you are not the wind in the orchard,
the plums on the counter,
or the house of cards.
And you are certainly not the pine-scented air.
There is no way you are the pine-scented air.

It is possible that you are the fish under the bridge,
maybe even the pigeon on the general's head,
but you are not even close
to being the field of cornflowers at dusk.

And a quick look in the mirror will show
that you are neither the boots in the corner
nor the boat asleep in its boathouse.

It might interest you to know,
speaking of the plentiful imagery of the world,
that I am the sound of rain on the roof.

I also happen to be the shooting star,
the evening paper blowing down an alley,
and the basket of chestnuts on the kitchen table.

I am also the moon in the trees
and the blind woman's teacup.
But don't worry, I am not the bread and the knife.
You are still the bread and the knife.
You will always be the bread and the knife,
not to mention the crystal goblet and—somehow—
        the wine.

Picking Grapes in an Abandoned Vineyard

LARRY LEVIS

Picking grapes alone in the late autumn sun—
A short, curved knife in my hand,
Its blade silver from so many sharpenings,
Its handle black.
I still have a scar where a friend
Sliced open my right index finger, once,
In a cutting shed—
The same kind of knife.
The grapes drop into the pan,
And the gnats swarm over them, as always.
Fifteen years ago,
I worked this row of vines beside a dozen
Families up from Mexico.
No one spoke English, or wanted to.
One woman, who made an omelet with a sheet of tin
And five, light blue quail eggs,
Had a voice full of dusk, and jail cells,
And bird calls. She spoke,
In Spanish, to no one, as they all did.
Their swearing was specific,
And polite.
I remember two of them clearly:
A man named Tea, six feet, nine inches tall
At the age of sixty-two,
Who wore white spats into downtown Fresno
Each Saturday night,
An alcoholic giant whom the women loved—

One chilled morning, they found him dead outside
The Rose Café . . .
And Angel Domínguez,
Who came to work for my grandfather in 1910,
And who saved for years to buy
Twenty acres of rotting, Thompson Seedless vines.
While the sun flared all one August,
He decided he was dying of a rare disease,
And spent his money and his last years
On specialists,
Who found nothing wrong.
Tea laughed, and, tipping back
A bottle of Muscatel, said: "Nothing's wrong.
You're just dying."
At seventeen, I discovered
Parlier, California, with its sad, topless bar,
And its one main street, and its opium.
I would stand still, and chalk my cue stick
In Johnny Paloroo' East Front Pool Hall, and watch
The room filling with tobacco smoke, as the sun set
Through one window.
Now all I hear are the vines rustling as I go
From one to the next,
The long canes holding up dry leaves, reddening,
So late in the year.
What the vines want must be this silence spreading
Over each town, over the dance halls and the dying parks,
And the police drowsing in their cruisers
Under the stars.
What the men who worked here wanted was
A drink strong enough
To let out what laughter they had.
I can still see the two of them:
Tea smiles and lets his yellow teeth shine—

191

While Angel, the serious one, for whom
Death was a rare disease,
Purses his lips, and looks down, as if
He is already mourning himself—
A soft, gray hat between his hands.
Today, in honor of them,
I press my thumb against the flat part of this blade,
And steady a bunch of red, Málaga grapes
With one hand,
The way they showed me, and cut—
And close my eyes to hear them laugh at me again,
And then, hearing nothing, no one,
Carry the grapes up to the solemn house,
Where I was born.

The Fine Printing on the Label
of a Bottle of Nonalcohol Beer

ADRIAN C. LOUIS

Then through an opening in the sky we were shown all the countries of the earth, and the camping grounds of our fathers since the beginning. All was there—the tipis, the ghosts of our fathers, and great herds of buffalo, and a country that smiled because it was rich and the white man was not there.
— MATO ANAHTAKA

The Redskins are winning
and I'm on the couch waiting for
the second half of their grunt-tussle
against the Chiefs to begin.
By ancient Indian habit,
I dash to the fridge for more suds.
For five years running now,
it's been this sad, nonalcohol beer
for me and my liver.
As usual, I read the health warning
before I drink the ersatz brew.
On the bottle's label, it says:

My brother, you are pouring
this illusion down your throat
because you are an alcoholic child
of alcoholic parents and they
were the alcoholic children
of your alcoholic grandparents.
My brother, oh, my brother
before your grandparents,

your great-grandparents
lived without firewater,
without the ghost of electricity,
without the white man's God
in bow and arrow old-time days.
Days of obsidian. Days of grace.
Days of buckskin. Days of grace.
Days of the war lance and the buffalo.
Days before your people learned
how to hotwire
the Great Spirit
with chemical prayers.

My Papa's Waltz

THEODORE ROETHKE

The whiskey on your breath
Could make a small boy dizzy;
But I hung on like death:
Such waltzing was not easy.

We romped until the pans
Slid from the kitchen shelf;
My mother's countenance
Could not unfrown itself.

The hand that held my wrist
Was battered on one knuckle;
At every step you missed
My right ear scraped a buckle.

You beat time on my head
With a palm caked hard by dirt,
Then waltzed me off to bed
Still clinging to your shirt.

SEASONINGS

*The amount of salt and pepper you want to use is your business. I don't
like to get in people's business. I have made everything in here and found
everything to be everything and everything came out very together.*
—VERTAMAE SMART-GROSVENOR,
Vibration Cooking

Ode to Salt

PABLO NERUDA

In the salt mines
I saw the salt
in this shaker.
I know you won't believe me,
but there
it sings,
the salt sings, the skin
of the salt mines
sings
with a mouth choking
on dirt.
Alone
when I heard
the voice
of salt,
I trembled
in the empty
desert.
Near Antofagasta
the whole
salted plain
shouts out
in its
cracked
voice
a pitiful
song.

Then in its caverns
jewels of rock salt, a mountain
of light buried under earth,
transparent cathedral,
crystal of the sea, oblivion
of the waves.

And now on each table
of the world
your agile
essence,
salt,
spreading
a vital luster
on
our food.
Preserver
of the ancient
stores in the holds
of ships, you were
the explorer
of the seas,
matter
foretold
in the secret, half-open
trails of foam.

Dust of water, the tongue
receives through you a kiss
from the marine night:
taste melds
your oceanity
into each rich morsel
and thus the least

wave
of the saltshaker
teaches us
not merely domestic purity
but also the essential flavor of the infinite.

Translated by Philip Levine

Ode to the Onion

PABLO NERUDA

Onion,
luminous flask,
your beauty formed
petal by petal,
crystal scales expanded you
and in the secrecy of the dark earth
your belly grew round with dew.
Under the earth
the miracle
happened
and when your clumsy
green stem appeared,
and your leaves were born
like swords
in the garden,
the earth heaped up her power
showing your naked transparency,
and as the remote sea
in lifting the breasts of Aphrodite
duplicating the magnolia,
so did the earth
make you,
onion
clear as a planet
and destined
to shine,
constant constellation,

round rose of water,
upon
the table
of the poor.

Generously
you undo
your globe of freshness
in the fervent consummation
of the cooking pot,
and the crystal shred
in the flaming heat of the oil
is transformed into a curled golden feather.

Then, too, I will recall how fertile
is your influence on the love of the salad,
and it seems that the sky contributes
by giving you the shape of hailstones
to celebrate your chopped brightness
on the hemispheres of a tomato.
But within reach
of the hands of the common people,
sprinkled with oil,
dusted
with a bit of salt,
you kill the hunger
of the day-laborer on his hard path.

Star of the poor,
fairy godmother
wrapped
in delicate
paper, you rise from the ground
eternal, whole, pure

like an astral seed,
and when the kitchen knife
cuts you, there arises
the only tear
without sorrow.

You make us cry without hurting us.
I have praised everything that exists,
but to me, onion, you are
more beautiful than a bird
of dazzling feathers,
heavenly globe, platinum goblet,
unmoving dance
of the snowy anemone

and the fragrance of the earth lives
in your crystalline nature.

Translated by Stephen Mitchell

Garlic

MARGARET GIBSON

Up from the depths
of the raised bed of earth
the stalks lift thin banners,
green in the wind.
The roots clasp the soil,
with the reluctance of lovers
letting go. But the earth
breaks open, warm as biscuits,
and the pale bulbs, crusted
with earth crumbs, enter
for the first time
air. Braided, on green pigtails
lashed to the chickenwire gate
of the garden, each bulb
dries to a rustle
weeks later, in my palm—
husky skins fine as rice paper,
veined like the leaf of a lily,
faintly varnished with gold.
Brittle papers that flake
when a thumb pries into
the cluster of cloves, prying
in and in, pinching the flesh
of a clove up under a nail—
and the odor! redolent,
a pungency in which pot roasts
and thick stews gather,

an aroma for eggplants and sesame
melding in a rich mystic kiss,
pure baba ganoush.
Let the feckless take it
odorless in capsules—
I simmer it in wine and tomatoes,
blend it with butter and basil,
lash the curved cloves
to a necklace I wear on my skin,
cold wolf-moon nights in the woods.
I stuff pillows with the skins,
rub the salad bowl of the lover's
body nightly with garlic,
breathe it out with the love cry,
let it rise, a nebula
into starry night skies . . .
for what if Dante were wrong
about paradise, the choirs
in their circular rows—what if
the celestial rose weren't petals
at all, but a commoner light,
a corona of cloves in their thin
garlic gowns, twisting up
into wicks that long to be lit,
and they are lit, flaming up
in the glory of God—
the God of the old myths
who leans over the fence
of the firmament, beyond pale
buds of new stars, leaning
our way, toward our own
common sod, sighing into it,
raising it, his breath
faintly garlic.

Fat

JANE KENYON

The doctor says it's better for my spine
this way—more fat, more estrogen.
Well, then! There was a time when a wife's
plump shoulders signified prosperity.

These days my fashionable friends
get by on seaweed milkshakes,
Pall Malls, and vitamin pills. Their clothes
hang elegantly from their clavicles.

As the evening news makes clear
the starving and the besieged maintain
the current standard of beauty without effort.

Whenever two or three gather together
the talk turns dreamily to sausages,
purple cabbages, black beans and rice,
noodles gleaming with cream, yams, and plums,
and chapati fried in ghee.

Specific Hunger

RODDY LUMSDEN

It's not enough to say a briny air
coasts off the gorge, that my downstairs neighbour
is basting a crisp-coated broiler,
that garlic and cardamom ghost on my hands
from the weekend's wondrous korma—

at times the craving is narrowed down,
shaved to a pill, hunted across fields to a den
where it surrenders and reveals itself
as chicken in soy sauce from that takeaway
long since demolished; the unlikely delicacy

of tinned risotto bubbled in its can;
sweet deep-fried sausages from a chip shop
on the back roads of Fife circa '71;
My eyes gloom up with lust, my mouth is rife,
the belly keening. The best of us mourn the loss

of such salt tongue blessings, part savour
and part pity, which we will not taste again:
musky pakora sauce subliming on my wrists
as I drifted home across The Meadows;
a lentil soup so true I knelt and wept.

Vindaloo in Merthyr Tydfil

LES MURRAY

The first night of my second voyage to Wales,
tired as rag from ascending the left cheek of Earth,
I nevertheless went to Merthyr in good company
and warm in neckclothing and speech in the Butcher's Arms
till Time struck us pintless, and Eddie Rees steamed in brick lanes
and under the dark of the White Tip we repaired shouting

to I think the Bengal. I called for curry, the hottest,
vain of my nation, proud of my hard mouth from childhood,
the kindly brown waiter wringing the hands of dissuasion
O vindaloo, sir! You sure you want vindaloo, sir?
But I cried Yes please, being too far in to go back,
the bright bells of Rhymney moreover sang in my brains.

Fair play, it was frightful. I spooned the chicken of Hell
in a sauce of rich yellow brimstone. The valley boys with me
tasting it, croaked to white Jesus. And only pride drove me,
forkful by forkful, observed by hot mangosteen eyes,
by all the carnivorous castes and gurus from Cardiff
my brilliant tears washing the unbelief of the Welsh.

Oh it was a ride on Watneys plunging red barrel
through all the burning ghats of most carnal ambition
and never again will I want such illumination
for three days on end concerning my own mortal coil
but I signed my plate in the end with a licked knife and fork
and green-and-gold spotted, I sang for my pains like the free
before I passed out among all the stars of Cilfynydd.

Hot

CRAIG ARNOLD

I'm cooking Thai—you bring the beer.
   The same order, although it's been a year

—friendships based on food are rarely stable.
   We should have left ours at the table

   where it began, and went to seed,
that appetite we shared, based less in need

than boredom—always the cheapest restaurants,
   Thai, Szechwan, taking our chance

with gangs and salmonella   what was hot?
   The five-starred curries? The penciled-out

   entrees?—the first to break a sweat
would leave the tip. I raise the knocker, let

it fall, once, twice, and when the door is opened
   I can't absorb, at first, what's happened

—face loosened a notch, eyes with a gloss
   of a fever left to run its course

too long, letting the unpropped skin collapse
   in a wrinkled heap. Only the lips

I recognize—dry, cracked, chapped
from licking. He looks as though he's slept

a week in the same clothes. *Come in, kick back,*
    he says, putting my warm six-pack

of Pale & Bitter into the fridge to chill.
    There's no music. I had to sell

the stereo to support my jones, he jokes,
    meaning the glut of good cookbooks

that cover one whole wall, in stacked milk crates
    six high, nine wide, two deep. He grates

        unripe papaya into a bowl,
fires off questions—*When did you finish school?*

    *Why not? Still single? Why? That dive
that served the ginger eels, did it survive?*

I don't get out much. Shall we go sometime?
    He squeezes the quarters of a lime

into the salad, adds a liberal squirt
    of chili sauce. *I won't be hurt*

*if you don't want seconds. It's not as hot
    as I would like to make it, but*

*you always were a bit of a lightweight.
    Here, it's finished, try a bite.*

He holds a forkful of the crisp
green shreds for me to take. I swallow, gasp,

choke—pins and needles shoot
through mouth and throat, a heat so absolute

as to seem freezing. I know better
not to wash it down with ice water

—it seems to cool, but only spreads the fire—
I can only bite my lip and swear

quietly to myself, so caught
up in our old routine—*What? This is hot?*

You're sweating. Care for another beer?
—it doesn't occur to me that he's sincere

until, my eyes watering, half in rage,
I open the door and find the fridge

stacked full with little jars of curry paste,
arranged by color, labels faced

carefully outward, some pushed back
to make room for the beer—no milk, no take-

out cartons of gelatinous chow mein,
no pickles rotting in green brine,

not even a jar of moldy mayonnaise.
—I see you're eating well these days,

I snap, pressing the beaded glass
of a beer bottle against my neck, face,

temples, anywhere it will hurt
enough to draw the fire out, and divert

attention from the fear that follows
close behind. . . . He stares at me, the hollows

under his eyes more prominent than ever.
    —*I don't eat much these days. The flavor*

has gone out of everything, almost.
    For the first time it's not a boast.

You know those small bird chili pods—the type
    you wear surgical gloves to chop,

    then soak your knife and cutting board
in vinegar? A month ago I scored

    a fresh bag—they were so ripe
I couldn't cut them warm, I had to keep

them frozen. I forget what I had meant
    to make, that night—I'd just cleaned

    the kitchen, wanted to fool around
with some old recipe I'd lost, and found

    jammed up behind a drawer—I had
maybe too much to drink. "Can't be that bad,"

*I remember thinking. "What's the fuss
about? It's not as if they're poisonous ..."*

*Those peppers, I ate them, raw—a big fistful
shoved in my mouth, swallowed whole,*

*and more, and more. It wasn't hard.
You hear of people getting their eyes charred*

to cinders, staring into an eclipse ...
He speaks so quickly, one of his lips

has cracked, leaks a trickle of blood
along his chin. . . . *I never understood.*

I try to speak, to offer some
small shocked rejoinder, but my mouth is numb

tingling, hurts to move   *I called in sick
next morning, said I'd like to take*

*time off. She thinks I've hit the bottle.
The high those peppers give me is more subtle*

*I'm lucid, I remember my full name,
my parents' birthdays, how to win a game*

*of chess in seven moves, why which and that
mean different things. But what we eat,*

*why, what it means, it's all been explained
—Take this curry, this fine-tuned*

balance of humors, coconut liquor thinned
    by broth, sour pulp of tamarind

    cut through by salt, set off by fragrant
galangal, ginger, basil, cilantro, mint,

the warp and woof of texture, aubergines
    that barely hold their shape, snap beans

    heaped on jasmine, basmati rice
—it's a lie, all of it—pretext—artifice

    —ornament—sugar-coating—for . . .
He stops, expressing heat from every pore

of his full face, unable to give vent
    to any more, and sits, silent,

    a whole minute. *You understand?*
Of course, I tell him. As he takes my hand

I can't help but notice the strength his grip
    has lost, as he lifts it to his lip,

presses it for a second, the torn flesh
    as soft, as tenuous, as ash,

    not in the least harsh or rough,
wreck of a mouth, that couldn't say *enough.*

Green Chile

JIMMY SANTIAGO BACA

I prefer red chile over my eggs
and potatoes for breakfast.
Red chile *ristras* decorate my door,
dry on my roof, and hang from eaves.
They lend open-air vegetable stands
historical grandeur, and gently swing
with an air of festive welcome.
I can hear them talking in the wind,
haggard, yellowing, crisp, rasping
tongues of old men, licking the breeze.

But grandmother loves green chile.
When I visit her,
she holds the green chile pepper
in her wrinkled hands.
Ah, voluptuous, masculine,
an air of authority and youth simmers
from its swan-neck stem, tapering to a flowery
collar, fermenting resinous spice.
A well-dressed gentleman at the door
my grandmother takes sensuously in her hand,
rubbing its firm glossed sides,
caressing the oily rubbery serpent,
with mouth-watering fulfillment,
fondling its curves with gentle fingers.
Its bearing magnificent and taut
as flanks of a tiger in mid-leap,

she thrusts her blade into
and cuts it open, with lust
on her hot mouth, sweating over the stove,
bandanna round her forehead,
mysterious passion on her face
as she serves me green chile con carne
between soft warm leaves of corn tortillas,
with beans and rice—her sacrifice
to her little prince.
I slurp from my plate
with last bit of tortilla, my mouth burns
and I hiss and drink a tall glass of cold water.

All over New Mexico, sunburned men and women
drive rickety trucks stuffed with gunny-sacks
of green chile, from Belen, Veguita, Willard, Estancia,
San Antonio y Socorro, from fields
to roadside stands, you see them roasting green chile
in screen-sided homemade barrels, and for a dollar a bag,
we relive this old, beautiful ritual again and again.

Yellow Light

GARRETT HONGO

One arm hooked around the frayed strap
of a tar-black patent-leather purse,
the other cradling something for dinner:
fresh bunches of spinach from a J-Town *yaoya*,
sides of split Spanish mackerel from Alviso's,
maybe a loaf of Langendorf; she steps
off the hissing bus at Olympic and Fig,
begins the three-block climb up the hill,
passing gangs of schoolboys playing war,
Japs against Japs, Chicanas chalking sidewalks
with the holy double-yoked crosses of hopscotch,
and the Korean grocer's wife out for a stroll
around the neighborhood of Hawaiian apartments
just starting to steam with cooking
and the anger of young couples coming home
from work, yelling at kids, flicking on
TV sets for the Wednesday Night Fights.

If it were May, hydrangeas and jacaranda
flowers in the streetside trees would be
blooming through the smog of late spring.
Wisteria in Masuda's front yard would be
shaking out the long tresses of its purple hair.
Maybe mosquitoes, moths, a few orange butterflies
settling on the lattice of monkey flowers
tangled in chain-link fences by the trash.

But this is October, and Los Angeles
seethes like a billboard under twilight
From used-car lots and the movie houses uptown,
long silver sticks of light probe the sky.
From the Miracle Mile, whole freeways away,
a brilliant fluorescence breaks out
and makes war with the dim squares
of yellow kitchen light winking on
in all the side streets of the Barrio.

She climbs up the two flights of flagstone
stairs to 201-B, the spikes of her high heels
clicking like kitchen knives on a cutting board,
props the groceries against the door,
fishes through memo pads, a compact,
empty packs of chewing gum, and finds her keys.

The moon then, cruising from behind
a screen of eucalyptus across the street,
covers everything, everything in sight,
in a heavy light like yellow onions.

Onions

WILLIAM MATTHEWS

How easily happiness begins by
dicing onions. A lump of sweet butter
slithers and swirls across the floor
of the sauté pan, especially if its
errant path crosses a tiny slick
of olive oil. Then a tumble of onions.

This could mean soup or risotto
or chutney (from the Sanskrit
chatni, to lick). Slowly the onions
go limp and then nacreous
and then what cookbooks call clear,
though if they were eyes you could see

clearly the cataracts in them.
It's true it can make you weep
to peel them, to unfurl and to tease
from the taut ball first the brittle,
caramel-colored and decrepit
papery outside layer, the least

recent the reticent onion
wrapped around its growing body,
for there's nothing to an onion
but skin, and it's true you can go on
weeping as you go on in, through
the moist middle skins, the sweetest

and thickest, and you can go on
in to the core, to the bud-like,
acrid, fibrous skins densely
clustered there, stalky and in-
complete, and these are the most
pungent, like the nuggets of nightmare

and rage and murmur animal
comfort that infant humans secrete.
This is the best domestic perfume.
You sit down to eat with a rumor
of onions still on your twice-washed
hands and lift to your mouth a hint

of a story about loam and usual
endurance. It's there when you clean up
and rinse the wine glasses and make
a joke, and you leave the minutest
whiff on it on the light switch,
later, when you climb the stairs.

Peeling Onions

ADRIENNE RICH

Only to have a grief
equal to all these tears!

There's not a sob in my chest.
Dry-hearted as Peer Gynt

I pare away, no hero,
merely a cook.

Crying was labor, once
when I'd good cause.
Walking, I felt my eyes like wounds
raw in my head,
so postal-clerks, I thought, must stare.
A dog's look, a cat's, burnt to my brain—
yet all that stayed
stuffed in my lungs like smog.

These old tears in the chopping-bowl.

Stepping Westward

DENISE LEVERTOV

What is green in me
darkens, muscadine.

If woman is inconstant,
good, I am faithful to

ebb and flow, I fall
in season and now

is a time of ripening.
If her part

is to be true,
a north star,

good, I hold steady
in the black sky

and vanish by day,
yet burn there

in blue or above
quilts of cloud.

There is no savor
more sweet, more salt

than to be glad to be
what, woman,

and who, myself,
I am, a shadow

that grows longer as the sun
moves, drawn out

on a thread of wonder.
If I bear burdens

they begin to be remembered
as gifts, goods, a basket

of bread that hurts
my shoulders but closes me

in fragrance. I can
eat as I go.

IV.
Sweet Summer

Do I dare to eat a peach?

—T. S. ELIOT

SHORT ORDERS

*I am proud to be an American. Because an American can eat
anything on the face of this earth as long as he has two pieces of bread.*
—BILL COSBY

Having a Coke with You

FRANK O'HARA

is even more fun than going to San Sebastian, Irún, Hendaye, Biarritz,
    Bayonne
or being sick to my stomach on the Travesera de Gracia in Barcelona
partly because in your orange shirt you look like a better happier
    St. Sebastian
partly because of my love for youth, partly because of your love for
    yoghurt
partly because of the fluorescent orange tulips around the birches
partly because of the secrecy our smiles take on before people and
    statuary
it is hard to believe when I'm with you that there can be anything
    as still
as solemn as unpleasantly definitive as statuary when right in front of
    it
in the warm New York 4 o'clock light we are drifting back and forth
between each other like a tree breathing through its spectacles

and the portrait show seems to have no faces in it at all, just paint
you suddenly wonder why in the world anyone ever did them
                                                            I look
at you and I would rather look at you than all the portraits in the
    world
except possibly for the *Polish Rider* occasionally and anyway it's in the
    Frick
which thank heavens you haven't gone to yet so we can go together
    the first time

and the fact that you move so beautifully more or less takes care of
          Futurism
just as at home I never think of the *Nude Descending a Staircase* or
at a rehearsal a single drawing of Leonardo or Michelangelo that used
          to wow me
and what good does all the research of the Impressionists do them
when they never got the right person to stand near the tree when the
          sun sank
or for that matter Marino Marini when he didn't pick the rider as
          carefully
as the horse
          it seems they were all cheated of some marvellous experience
which is not going to go wasted on me which is why I'm telling you
          about it

from Letters to Wendy's

JOE WENDEROTH

JULY 3, 1996

Today I bought a small Frosty. This may not seem
significant, but the fact is: I'm lactose intolerant. Purchasing
a small Frosty, then, is no different than hiring someone to
beat me. No different in essence. The only difference,
which may or may not be essential, is that, during my
torture, I am gazing upon your beautiful employees.

JULY 6, 1996

I was so high on Sudafed and whiskey today that I couldn't
eat. I got a Coke—actually five Cokes, as I could refill for
free. It's times like this—dehydrated, exhausted, unable to
imagine home—that your plastic seats, your quiet
understandable room, set beside but not quite overlooking
the source of real value, offer me a tragedy small enough to
want to endure.

AUGUST 19, 1996

Today I was thinking that it might be nice to be able, in
one's last days, to move into a Wendy's. Perhaps a Wendy's
life-support system could even be created and given a
Wendy's slant; liquid fries, for instance, and burgers and
Frosties continually dripped into one's vegetable dream
locus. It would intensify the visits of the well, too, to see
that such a care is being taken for their destiny.

NOVEMBER 16, 1996

It's good, this not knowing anyone's name. The employees have name-tags, but no one believes them. Their anonymity is far too obvious. How monstrous to introduce oneself to one's register person! How useless, how wearying, that information is! Only the shouted names of children make sense here, denoting not a person but a drifting off, a subversive fascination.

FEBRUARY 14, 1997

It has taken me this long to confess that I am not a fan of the salad bar. That is, to *openly* confess it. Surely my silence on the matter has created an impression already. I suppose I've been ashamed to speak. I have this sense that in speaking I will be led to something embarrassing, something at odds with the uniquely liberal persona I prance about in. This, though, this letter, is a good first step.

JULY 9, 1997

I'm so sorry for everything I've said. I'd take it back if I could. I am willing to admit that, in some sense, these descriptions of my visits have obscured the sufficiency of the meals I've had. I will not admit, however, that sufficiency is something I could be reasonably expected to live with. That is, I am truly sorry, but an insufficient meal *is* available, and nothing else tastes as sweet.

Woe

CAMPBELL MCGRATH

Consider the human capacity for suffering,
our insatiable appetite for woe.
I do not say this lightly
but the sandwiches at Subway
suck. Foaming lettuce,
mayo like rancid bear grease,
meat the color of a dead dog's tongue.
Yet they are consumed
by the millions
and by the tens of millions.
So much for the food. The rest
I must pass over in silence.

Food

BRENDA HILLMAN

In a side booth at MacDonald's before your music class
you go up and down in your seat like an arpeggio
under the poster of the talking hamburger:
two white eyes rolling around in the top bun, the thin
patty of beef imitating the tongue of its animal nature.
You eat merrily. I watch the Oakland mommies,
trying to understand what it means to be "single."

Across from us, females of all ages surround the birthday girl.
Her pale lace and insufficient being
can't keep them out of her circle.
Stripes of yellow and brown all over the place.
The poor in spirit have started to arrive,
the one with thick midwestern braids twisted like thought
on her head; usually she brings her mother.
This week, no mother. She mouths her words anyway
across the table, space-mama, time-mama,
mama who should be there.

Families in line: imagine all this
translated by the cry of time moving through us,
this place a rubble. The gardens new generations
will plant in this spot, and the food will go on
in another order. This thought cheers me immensely.
That we will be here together, you still seven,

bending over the crops pretending to be royalty,
that the huge woman with one blind eye
and dots like eyes all over her dress
will also be there, eating with pleasure
as she eats now, right up to the tissue paper,
peeling it back like bright exotic petals.

⁓

Last year, on the sun-spilled deck in Marin
we ate grapes with the Russians;
the KGB man fingered them quickly and dutifully,
then, in a sad tone to us
"We must not eat them so fast,
we wait in line so long for these," he said.

⁓

The sight of food going into a woman's mouth
made Byron sick. Food is a metaphor for existence.
When Mr. Egotistical Sublime, eating the pasta,
poked one finger into his mouth, he made a sound.
For some, the curve of the bell pepper
seems sensual but it can worry you,
the slightly greasy feel of it.

⁓

The place I went with your father had an apartment to the left, and in
        the window, twisted like a huge bowtie,
an old print bedspread. One day, when I looked over,
someone was watching us, a young girl.
The waiter had just brought the first thing:
an orange with an avocado sliced up CCCC
in an oil of forceful herbs. I couldn't eat it.
The girl's face stood for something
and from it, a little mindless daylight was reflected.

The businessmen at the next table
were getting off on each other and the young chardonnay.
Their briefcases leaned against their ankles.
I watched the young girl's face because for an instant
I had seen your face there,
unterrified, unhungry, and a little disdainful.
Then the waiter brought the food,
bands of black seared into it like the memory of a cage.

—

You smile over your burger, chattering brightly.
So often, at our sunny kitchen table,
hearing the mantra of the refrigerator,
I've thought there was nothing I could do but feed you;
and I've always loved the way you eat,
you eat selfishly, humming, bending
the french fries to your will, your brown eyes
spotting everything: the tall boy
who has come in with his mother, repressed rage
in espadrilles, and now carries the tray for her.
Oh this is fun, says the mother,
You stand there with mommy's purse.
And he stands there smiling after her,
holding all the patience in the world.

Breakfast

MINNIE BRUCE PRATT

Rush hour, and the short order cook lobs breakfast
sandwiches, silverfoil softballs, up and down the line.
We stand until someone says, *Yes?* The next person behind
breathes hungrily. The cashier's hands never stop. He shouts:
Where's my double double? We help. We eliminate all verbs.
The superfluous *want, need, give* they already know. Nothing's left
but *stay* or *go*, and a few things like *bread*. No one can stay long,
not even the stolid man in blue-hooded sweats, head down, eating,
his work boots powdered with cement dust like snow that never
melts.

Night Waitress

LYNDA HULL

Reflected in the plate glass, the pies
look like clouds drifting off my shoulder.
I'm telling myself my face has character,
not beauty. It's my mother's Slavic face.
She washed the floor on hands and knees
below the Black Madonna, praying
to her god of sorrows and visions
who's not here tonight when I lay out the plates,
small planets, the cups and moons of saucers.
At this hour the men all look
as if they'd never had mothers.
They do not see me. I bring the cups.
I bring the silver. There's the man
who leans over the jukebox nightly
pressing the combinations
of numbers. I would not stop him
if he touched me, but it's only songs
of risky love he leans into. The cook sings
with the jukebox, a moan and sizzle
into the grill. On his forehead
a tattoed cross furrows,
diminished when he frowns. He sings words
dragged up from the bottom of his lungs.
I want a song that rolls
through the night like a big Cadillac
past factories to the refineries
squatting on the bay, round and shiny

as the coffee urn warming my palm.
Sometimes when coffee cruises my mind
visiting the most remote way stations,
I think of my room as a calm arrival
each book and lamp in its place. The calendar
on my wall predicts no disaster
only another white square waiting
to be filled like the desire that fills
jail cells, the cold arrest
that makes me stare out the window or want
to try every bar down the street.
When I walk out of here in the morning
my mouth is bitter with sleeplessness.
Men surge to the factories and I'm too tired
to look. Fingers grip lunch box handles,
belt buckles gleam, wind riffles my uniform
and it's not romantic when the sun unlids
the end of the avenue. I'm fading
in the morning's insinuations
collecting in the crevices of the building,
in wrinkles, in every fault
of this frail machinery.

1953

JACK GILBERT

All night in the Iowa café. Friday night
and the farm boys with their pay.
Fine bodies and clean faces. All of them
proud to be drunk. No meanness,
just energy. At the next table, they talked
cars for hours, friends coming and going,
hollering over. The one with the heavy face
and pale hair kept talking about the Chevy
he had years ago and how it could
take everything in second.
Moaning that he should never have sold it.
Didn't he show old Hank? Bet your ass!
That Fourth of July when Shelvadeen
got too much patriotism and beer
and gave some to everybody
down by the river. Hank so mad because
I left him like he was standing still.
Best car that ever was, and never should have
let it go. Tears falling on his eggs.

The Latin Deli: An Ars Poetica

JUDITH ORTIZ COFER

Presiding over a formica counter,
plastic Mother and Child magnetized
to the top of an ancient register,
the heady mix of smells from the open bins
of dried codfish, the green plantains
hanging in stalks like votive offerings,
she is the Patroness of Exiles,
a woman of no-age who was never pretty,
who spends her days selling canned memories
while listening to the Puerto Ricans complain
that it would be cheaper to fly to San Juan
than to buy a pound of Bustelo coffee here,
and to Cubans perfecting their speech
of a "glorious return" to Havana—where no one
has been allowed to die and nothing to change until then;
to Mexicans who pass through, talking lyrically
of *dólares* to be made in El Norte—
                              all wanting the comfort
of spoken Spanish, to gaze upon the family portrait
of her plain wide face, her ample bosom
resting on her plump arms, her look of maternal interest
as they speak to her and each other
of their dreams and their disillusions—
how she smiles understanding,
when they walk down the narrow aisles of her store
reading the labels of packages aloud, as if
they were the names of lost lovers: *Suspiros,*

Merengues, the stale candy of everyone's childhood.
                                         She spends her days
slicing *jamón y queso* and wrapping it in wax paper
tied with string: plain ham and cheese
that would cost less at the A&P, but it would not satisfy
the hunger of the fragile old man lost in the folds
of his winter coat, who brings her lists of items
that he reads to her like poetry, or the others,
whose needs she must divine, conjuring up products
from places that now exist only in their hearts—
closed ports she must trade with.

Coca-Cola and Coco Frío

MARTÍN ESPADA

On his first visit to Puerto Rico,
island of family folklore,
the fat boy wandered
from table to table
with his mouth open.
At every table, some great-aunt
would steer him with cool spotted hands
to a glass of Coca-Cola.
One even sang to him, in all the English
she could remember, a Coca-Cola jingle
from the forties. He drank obediently, though
he was bored with this potion, familiar
from soda fountains in Brooklyn.

Then at a roadside stand off the beach, the fat boy
opened his mouth to coco frío, a coconut
chilled, then scalped by a machete
so that a straw could inhale the clear milk.
The boy tilted the green shell overhead
and drooled coconut milk down his chin;
suddenly, Puerto Rico was not Coca-Cola
or Brooklyn, and neither was he.

For years afterward, the boy marveled at an island
where the people drank Coca-Cola
and sang jingles from World War II
in a language they did not speak,

while so many coconuts in the trees
sagged heavy with milk, swollen
and unsuckled.

A Step Away from Them

FRANK O'HARA

It's my lunch hour, so I go
for a walk among the hum-colored
cabs. First, down the sidewalk
where laborers feed their dirty
glistening torsos sandwiches
and Coca-Cola, with yellow helmets
on. They protect them from falling
bricks, I guess. Then onto the
avenue where skirts are flipping
above heels and blow up over
grates. The sun is hot, but the
cabs stir up the air. I look
at bargains in wristwatches. There
are cats playing in sawdust.
                          On
to Times Square, where the sign
blows smoke over my head, and higher
the waterfall pours lightly. A
Negro stands in a doorway with a
toothpick, languorously agitating.
A blonde chorus girl clicks: he
smiles and rubs his chin. Everything
suddenly hongs: it is 12:40 of
a Thursday.
            Neon in daylight is a
great pleasure, as Edwin Denby would
write, as are light bulbs in daylight.

I stop for a cheeseburger at JULIET'S
CORNER. Giulietta Masina, wife of
Federico Fellini, è bell' attrice.
And chocolate malted. A lady in
foxes on such a day puts her poodle
in a cab.
There are several Puerto
Ricans on the avenue today, which
makes it beautiful and warm. First
Bunny died, then John Latouche,
then Jackson Pollock. But is the
earth as full as life was full, of them?
And one has eaten and one walks,
past the magazines with nudes
and the posters for BULLFIGHT and
the Manhattan Storage Warehouse,
which they'll soon tear down. I
used to think they had the Armory
Show there.
A glass of papaya juice
and back to work. My heart is in my
pocket, it is Poems by Pierre Reverdy.

Love Is Not an Emergency

ERIN BELIEU

more like weather, that is
ubiquitous, true

or false spring: the ambivalence
we have for any picnic—

flies ass-up in the Jell-O;
    the soft bulge of thunderheads.

Right now, the man in the booth
next to me
    at the Nautilus Diner,
        Madison, New Jersey,

is crying, but looks up
    to order the famous disco fries.

So the world's saddest thing shakes you
    like a Magic 8 Ball;

and before him, the minstrel
    who smeared on love's blackface, rattling

his damage like a tambourine.

I have been the deadest nag
    limping circles around

the paddock, have flown to beady pieces,

sick as the tongue of mercury
    at the thermometer's tip.

But let's admit there's a pleasure, too,
in living as we do,

    like two-strike felons who smile
for the security cameras,

like love's first responders,

stuffing our kits with enhancement
    pills, Zig Zags, and Power Ball cards

I read: to great is the cognate for
    regret, to weep, but welcome
      our weeping,

because "we grant the name of love
    to something less than love";

because we all have to eat.

—For A. C.

Degrees of Gray in Philipsburg

RICHARD HUGO

You might come here Sunday on a whim.
Say your life broke down. The last good kiss
you had was years ago. You walk these streets
laid out by the insane, past hotels
that didn't last, bars that did, the tortured try
of local drivers to accelerate their lives.
Only churches are kept up. The jail
turned 70 this year. The only prisoner
is always in, not knowing what he's done.

The principal supporting business now
is rage. Hatred of the various grays
the mountain sends, hatred of the mill,
The Silver Bill repeal, the best liked girls
who leave each year for Butte. One good
restaurant and bars can't wipe the boredom out.
The 1907 boom, eight going silver mines,
a dance floor built on springs—
all memory resolves itself in gaze,
in panoramic green you know the cattle eat
or two stacks high above the town,
two dead kilns, the huge mill in collapse
for fifty years that won't fall finally down.

Isn't this your life? That ancient kiss
still burning out your eyes? Isn't this defeat
so accurate, the church bell simply seems

a pure announcement: ring and no one comes?
Don't empty houses ring? Are magnesium
and scorn sufficient to support a town,
not just Philipsburg, but towns
of towering blondes, good jazz and booze
the world will never let you have
until the town you came from dies inside?

Say no to yourself. The old man, twenty
when the jail was built, still laughs
although his lips collapse. Someday soon,
he says, I'll go to sleep and not wake up.
You tell him no. You're talking to yourself.
The car that brought you here still runs.
The money you buy lunch with,
no matter where it's mined, is silver
and the girl who serves you food
is slender and her red hair lights the wall.

DINNER FOR TWO

Cooking is like love; it should be entered into with abandon or not at all.

—JULIA CHILD

Interlude

AMY LOWELL

When I have baked white cakes
And grated green almonds to spread on them;
When I have picked the green crowns from the strawberries
And piled them, cone-pointed, in a blue and yellow platter;
When I have smoothed the seam of the linen I have been working;
What then?
To-morrow it will be the same:
Cakes and strawberries,
And needles in and out of cloth
If the sun is beautiful on bricks and pewter,
How much more beautiful is the moon,
Slanting down the gauffered branches of a plum-tree;
The moon
Wavering across a bed of tulips;
The moon,
Still,
Upon your face.
You shine, Beloved,
You and the moon.
But which is the reflection?
The clock is striking eleven.
I think, when we have shut and barred the door,
The night will be dark
Outside.

Putting in the Seed

ROBERT FROST

You come to fetch me from my work tonight
When supper's on the table, and we'll see
If I can leave off burying the white
Soft petals fallen from the apple tree
(Soft petals, yes, but not so barren quite,
Mingled with these, smooth bean and wrinkled pea;)
And go along with you ere you lose sight
Of what you came for and become like me,
Slave to a springtime passion for the earth.
How Love burns through the Putting in the Seed
On through the watching for that early birth
When, just as the soil tarnishes with weed,
The sturdy seedling with arched body comes
Shouldering its way and shedding the earth crumbs.

Poem with a Cucumber in It

ROBERT HASS

Sometimes from this hillside just after sunset
The rim of the sky takes on a tinge
Of the palest green, like the flesh of a cucumber
When you peel it carefully.

In Crete once, in the summer,
When it was still hot at midnight,
We sat in a tavern by the water
Watching the squid boats rocking in the moonlight,
Drinking retsina and eating salads
Of cool, chopped cucumber and yogurt and a little dill.

A hint of salt, something like starch, something
Like an attar of grasses or green leaves
On the tongue is the tongue
And the cucumber
Evolving toward each other.

Since *cumbersome* is a word,
Cumber must have been a word,
Lost to us now, and even then,
For a person feeling encumbered,
It must have felt orderly and right-minded
To stand at a sink and slice a cucumber.

If you think I am going to make
A sexual joke in this poem, you are mistaken.

In the old torment of the earth
When the fires were cooling and disposing themselves
Into granite and limestone and serpentine and shale,
It is possible to imagine that, under yellowish chemical clouds,
The molten froth, having burned long enough,
Was already dreaming of release,
And that the dream, dimly
But with increasingly distinctness, took the form
Of water, and that it was then, still more dimly, that it imagined
The dark green skin and opal green flesh of cucumbers.

from Tender Buttons

GERTRUDE STEIN

APPLE

Apple plum, carpet steak, seed clam, colored wine, calm seen, cold cream, best shake, potato, potato and no no gold work with pet, a green seen is called bake and change sweet is bready, a little piece a little piece please.

A little piece please. Cane again to the presupposed and ready eucalyptus tree, count out sherry and ripe plates and little corners of a kind of ham. This is use.

CUPS

A single example of excellence is in the meat. A bent stick is surging and might all might is mental. A grand clothes is searching out a candle not that wheatly not that by more than an owl and a path. A ham is proud of cocoanut.

A cup is neglected by being all in size. It is a handle and meadows and sugar any sugar.

A cup is neglected by being full in size. It shows no shade, in come little wood cuts and blessing and nearly not that not with a wild bought in, not at all so polite, not nearly so behind.

Cups crane in. They need a pet oyster, they need it so hoary and nearly choice. The best slam is utter. Nearly be freeze.

Why is a cup a stir and a behave. Why is it so seen.

A cup is readily shaded, it has in between no sense that is to say music, memory, musical memory.

Peanuts blame, a half sand is holey and nearly.

RHUBARB

Rhubarb is susan not susan not seat in bunch toys not wild and laughable not in little places not in neglect and vegetable not in fold coal age not please.

CUSTARD

Custard is this. It has aches, aches when. Not to be. Not to be narrowly. This makes a whole little hill.

It is better than a little thing that has mellow real mellow. It is better than lakes whole lakes, it is better than seeding.

ASPARAGUS

Asparagus in a lean in a lean to hot. This makes it art and it is wet wet weather wet weather wet.

BUTTER

Boom in boom in, butter. Leave a grain and show it, show it. I spy.

It is a need it is a need that a flower a state flower. It is a need that a state rubber. It is a need that a state rubber is sweet and sight and a swelled stretch. It is a need. It is a need that state rubber.

Wood a supply. Clean little keep a strange, estrange on it.

Make a little white, no and not with pit, pit on in within.

SALAD

It is a winning cake.

ORANGE

Why is a feel oyster an egg stir. Why is it orange centre.

A show at tick and loosen loosen it so to speak sat.

It was an extra leaker with a see spoon, it was an extra licker with a see spoon.

SALAD DRESSING AND AN ARTICHOKE

Please pale hot, please cover rose, please acre in the red stranger, please butter all the beef-steak with regular feel faces.

SALAD DRESSING AND AN ARTICHOKE

It was please it was please carriage cup in an ice-cream, in an ice-cream it was too bended bended with scissors and all this time. A whole is inside a part, a part does go away, a hole is red leaf. No choice was where there was and a second and a second.

Ode to Okra

MARY SWANDER

Mumbo, jumbo, pot-full-of-gumbo, o sweet okra,
red stem, pink blossom, only plant in the garden
to survive this summer's heat, wilt, grasshopper drought.

And there is no cure for this plague:
guinea hens, traps, sprays, hand-picking won't stop
these insects from stripping leaves,
chewing through the screen door.

Rain fifteen inches down, their eggs never drowning,
these bugs just keep on fucking—two, three, four
generations at once hovering on the fence,
waiting to begin their chomping.

And there is no help for the poor
tomatoes, potatoes, lettuce, turnips, squash.
They've all collapsed into mush.

All but my beautiful, ugly okra.
Seed pods: sliced, diced, rolled in corn meal,
fried in a pan. Cut up and dropped into soups,
stew pots in the winter to stretch further.

Take me in, sweet meat, teach me the secret
of your stalks, eye high by the Fourth of July.
Heal me with the nod of your leaves,

the deep veins and lobes, bundles of fibers,
the thin layer of skin covering your bud scars,
the shimmer of each new flower.

A Supermarket in California

ALLEN GINSBERG

What thoughts I have of you tonight, Walt Whitman, for I walked down the sidestreets under the trees with a headache self-conscious looking at the full moon.

In my hungry fatigue, and shopping for images, I went into the neon fruit supermarket, dreaming of your enumerations!

What peaches and what penumbras? Whole families shopping at night! Aisles full of husbands! Wives in the avocados, babies in the tomatoes!—and you, García Lorca, what were you doing down by the watermelons?

I saw you, Walt Whitman, childless, lonely old grubber, poking among the meats in the refrigerator and eyeing the grocery boys.

I heard you asking questions of each: Who killed the pork chops? What price bananas? Are you my Angel?

I wandered in and out of the brilliant stacks of cans following you, and followed in my imagination by the store detective.

We strode down the open corridors together in our solitary fancy tasting artichokes, possessing every frozen delicacy, and never passing the cashier.

Where are we going, Walt Whitman? The doors close in an hour. Which way does your beard point tonight?

(I touch your book and dream of our odyssey in the supermarket and feel absurd.)

Will we walk all night through solitary streets? The trees add shade to shade, lights out in the houses, we'll both be lonely.

Will we stroll dreaming of the lost America of love past blue automobiles in driveways, home to our silent cottage?

Ah, dear father, graybeard, lonely old courage-teacher, what America did you have when Charon quit poling his ferry and you got out on a smoking bank and stood watching the boat disappear on the black waters of Lethe?

Susie Asado

GERTRUDE STEIN

Sweet sweet sweet sweet sweet tea.
    Susie Asado.
Sweet sweet sweet sweet sweet tea.
    Susie Asado.
Susie Asado which is a told tray sure.
A lean on the shoe this means slips slips hers.
When the ancient light grey is clean it is yellow, it is a
silver seller.
This is a please this is a please there are the saids to jelly.
These are the wets these say the sets to leave a crown to
Incy.
    Incy is short for incubus.
    A pot. A pot is a beginning of a rare bit of trees. Trees
tremble, the old vats are in bobbles, bobbles which shade and
shove and render clean, render clean must.
    Drink pups.
    Drink pups drink pups lease a sash hold, see it shine and
a bobolink has pins. It shows a nail.
    What is a nail. A nail is unison.
Sweet sweet sweet sweet sweet tea.

Squid

MICHAEL C. BLUMENTHAL

So this is love:

How your grimace at the sight
of these fish; how I pull
(forefinger, then thumb)
the fins and tails from the heads,
slice the tentacles from the accusing eyes.

And then how I pile the silvery ink sacs
into the sieve like old fillings, heap
the entrails and eyes on a towel in the corner;
and how you sauté the onions and garlic,
how they turn soft and transparent, lovely
in their own way, and how you turn to me
and say, simply, *isn't this fun, isn't it?*

And something tells me this all has to do
with love, perhaps even more than lust
or happiness have to do with love:
How the fins slip easily from the tails,
how I peel the membranes from the fins
and cones like a man peeling his body
from a woman after love, how these
ugly squid diminish in grotesqueness
and all nausea reduces, finally, to a hunger
for what is naked and approachable,

tangible and delicious.

Mushrooms

MARY OLIVER

Rain, and then
the cool pursed
lips of the wind
draw them
out of the ground—
red and yellow skulls
pummeling upward
through leaves,
through grasses,
through sand: astonishing
in their suddenness,
their quietude,
their wetness, they appear
on fall mornings, some
balancing in the earth
on one hoof
packed with poison,
others billowing
chunkily, and delicious—
those who know
walk out to gather, choosing
the benign from flocks
of glitterers, sorcerers
russulas,
panther caps,
shark-white death angels
in their torn veils
looking innocent as sugar

but full of paralysis:
to eat
is to stagger down
fast as mushrooms themselves
when they are done being perfect
and overnight
slide back under the shining
fields of rain.

Mushrooms

SYLVIA PLATH

Overnight, very
Whitely, discreetly,
Very quietly

Our toes, our noses
Take hold on the loam,
Acquire the air.

Nobody sees us,
Stops us, betrays us;
The small grains make room.

Soft fists insist on
Heaving the needles,
The leafy bedding,

Even the paving.
Our hammers, our rams,
Earless and eyeless,

Perfectly voiceless,
Widen the crannies,
Shoulder through holes. We

Diet on water,
On crumbs of shadow,
Bland-mannered, asking

Little or nothing.
So many of us!
So many of us!

We are shelves, we are
Tables, we are meek,
We are edible,

Nudgers and shovers
In spite of ourselves.
Our kind multiplies:

We shall by morning
Inherit the earth.
Our foot's in the door.

It Was Like This: You Were Happy

JANE HIRSHFIELD

It was like this:
you were happy, then you were sad,
then happy again, then not.

It went on.
You were innocent or you were guilty.
Actions were taken, or not.

At times you spoke, at other times you were silent.
Mostly, it seems you were silent—what could you say?

Now it is almost over.

Like a lover, your life bends down and kisses your life.

It does this not in forgiveness
between you, there is nothing to forgive—
but with the simple nod of a baker at the moment
he sees the bread is finished with transformation.

Eating, too, is a thing now only for others.

It doesn't matter what they will make of you
or your days: they will be wrong,
they will miss the wrong woman, miss the wrong man,
all the stories they tell will be tales of their own invention.

Your story was this: you were happy, then you were sad,
you slept, you awakened.
Sometimes you ate roasted chestnuts, sometimes persimmons.

A Sweetening All Around Me as It Falls

JANE HIRSHFIELD

Even generous August,
only a child's scribblings
on thick black paper, in smudgeable chalk—
even the ripening tomatoes, even the roses,
blowsy, loosing their fragrance of black tea.
A winter light held this morning's apples
as they fell, sweet, streaked by one touch
of the careless brush, appling to earth.
The seeds so deep inside they carry that cold.
Is this why some choose solitude, to rise
that small bit further, unencumbered by love of earth,
as the branches, lighter, kite now a little higher
on gold air? But the apples love earth and falling,
lose themselves in it as much as they can at first touch
and then, with time and rain, at last completely:
to be that bone-like One that shines unleafed in winter rain,
all black and glazed with not the pendant gold of
necklaced summer but the ice-color mirroring starlight
when the earth is empty and dark and knows nothing of apples.
Seed-black of the paper, seed-black of the waiting heart—
December's shine, austere and fragile, carves the visible tree.
But today, cut deep in last plums, in yellow pears,
in second flush of roses, in the warmth of an hour, now late,
as drunk on heat as the girl who long ago vanished into green trees,
fold that loneliness, one moment, two, love, back into your arms.

Holy Thursday

PAUL MULDOON

They're kindly here, to let us linger so late,
Long after the shutters are up.
A waiter glides from the kitchen with a plate
Of stew, or some thick soup,

And settles himself at the next table but one.
We know, you and I, that it's over,
That something or other has come between
Us, whatever we are, or were.

The waiter swabs his plate with bread
And drains what's left of his wine,
Then rearranges, one by one,
The knife, the fork, the spoon, the napkin,
The table itself, the chair he's simply borrowed,
And smiles, and bows to his own absence.

Never May the Fruit Be Plucked

EDNA ST. VINCENT MILLAY

Never, never may the fruit be plucked from the bough
And gathered into barrels.
He that would eat of love must eat it where it hangs.
Though the branches bend like reeds,
Though the ripe fruit splash in the grass or wrinkle on the tree,
He that would eat of love may bear away with him
Only what his belly can hold,
Nothing in the apron,
Nothing in the pockets.
Never, never may the fruit be gathered from the bough
And harvested in barrels.
The winter of love is a cellar of empty bins,
In an orchard soft with rot.

FORBIDDEN FRUIT

*Our diet, like that of the birds, must answer to the season. This is the season
of west-looking, watery fruits. In the dog-days we come near to sustaining
our lives on watermelon juice alone, like those who have fevers. I know of
no more agreeable and nutritious food at this season than bread and butter and
melons, and you need not be afraid of eating too much of the latter.*

—HENRY DAVID THOREAU

"WILD FRUITS"

This Is Just to Say

WILLIAM CARLOS WILLIAMS

I have eaten
the plums
that were in
the icebox

and which
you were probably
saving
for breakfast

Forgive me
they were delicious
so sweet
and so cold

The Plum's Heart

GARY SOTO

I've climbed in trees
To eat, and climbed
Down to look about
This world, mouth red
From plums that were
Once clouds in March
—rain I mean, that
Pitiless noise against
Leaves and branches.
Father once lifted me
Into one, and from
A distance I might
Have been a limb,
Moving a little heavier
Than most but a limb
All the same. My hands
Opened like mouths,
The juice running
Without course down
My arms, as I stabbed
For plums, bunched
Or half-hidden behind
Leaves. A bird fluttered
From there, a single
Leaf cutting loose,
And gnats like smoke
Around a bruised plum.

I climbed searching
For those red globes,
And with a sack filled,
I called for father
To catch—father
Who would disappear
Like fruit at the end
Of summer, from a neck
Wound some say—blood
Running like the juice
Of these arms. I
Twisted the throat
Of the sack, tossed
It, and started down
To father, his mouth
Already red and grinning
Like the dead on their
Rack of blackness.
When I jumped, he was
Calling, arms open,
The sack at his feet
For us, the half-bitten,
Who bring on the flies.

Grape Sherbet

RITA DOVE

The day? Memorial.
After the grill
Dad appears with his masterpiece—
swirled snow, gelled light.
We cheer. The recipe's
a secret and he fights
a smile, his cap turned up
so the bib resembles a duck.

That morning we galloped
through the grassed-over mounds
and named each stone
for a lost milk tooth. Each dollop
of sherbet, later,
is a miracle,
like salt on a melon that makes it sweeter.

Everyone agrees— it's wonderful!
It's just how we imagined lavender
would taste. The diabetic grandmother
stares from the porch,
a torch
of pure refusal.

We thought no one was lying
there under our feet,
we thought it

was a joke. I've been trying
to remember the taste,
but it doesn't exist.
Now I see why
you bothered,
father.

Meditation on a Grapefruit

CRAIG ARNOLD

To wake when all is possible
before the agitations of the day
have gripped you
          To come to the kitchen
and peel a little basketball
for breakfast
         To tear the husk
like cotton padding   a cloud of oil
misting out of its pinprick pores
clean and sharp as pepper
         To ease
each pale pink section out of its case
so carefully   without breaking
a single pearly cell
         To slide each piece
into a cold blue china bowl
the juice pooling   until the whole
fruit is divided from its skin
and only then to eat
         so sweet
         a discipline
precisely pointless   a devout
involvement of the hands and senses
a pause   a little emptiness

each year harder to live within
each year harder to live without

Grapefruit

GERALD STERN

I'm eating breakfast even if it means standing
in front of the sink and tearing at the grapefruit,
even if I'm leaning over to keep the juices
away from my chest and stomach and even if a spider
is hanging from my ear and a wild flea
is crawling down my leg. My window is wavy
and dirty. There is a wavy tree outside
with pitiful leaves in front of the rusty fence
and there is a patch of useless rhubarb, the leaves
bent over, the stalks too large and bitter for eating,
and there is some lettuce and spinach too old for picking
beside the rhubarb. This is the way the saints
ate, only they dug for thistles, the feel
of thorns in the throat it was a blessing, my pity
it knows no bounds. There is a thin tomato plant
inside a rolled-up piece of wire, the worms
are already there, the birds are bored. In time
I'll stand beside the rolled-up fence with tears
of gratitude in my eyes. I'll hold a puny
pinched tomato in my open hand,
I'll hold it to my lips. Blessed art Thou,
King of tomatoes, King of grapefruit. The thistle
must have juices, there must be a trick. I hate
to say it but I'm thinking if there is a saint
in our time what will he be, and what will he eat?
I hated rhubarb, all that stringy sweetness—
a fake applesauce—I hated spinach,

always with egg and vinegar, I hated
oranges when they were quartered, that was the signal
for castor oil—aside from the peeled navel
I love the Florida cut in two. I bend
my head forward, my chin is in the air,
I hold my right hand off to the side, the pinkie
is waving; I am back again at the sink;
oh loneliness, I stand at the sink, my garden
is dry and blooming, I love my lettuce, I love
my cornflowers, the sun is doing it all,
the sun and a little dirt and a little water.
I lie on the ground out there, there is one yard
between the house and the tree; I am more calm there
looking back at this window, looking up
a little at the sky, a blue passageway
with smears of white—and grey—a bird crossing
from berm to berm, from ditch to ditch, another use,
a wild highway, a wild skyway, a flock
of little ones to make me feel gay, they fly
down the thruway, I move my eyes back and forth
to see them appear and disappear, I stretch
my neck, a kind of exercise. Ah sky,
my breakfast is over, my lunch is over, the wind
has stopped, it is the hour of deepest thought.
Now I brood, I grimace, how quickly the day goes,
how full it is of sunshine, and wind, how many
smells there are, how gorgeous is the distant
sound of dogs, and engines—Blessed art Thou,
Lord of the falling leaf, Lord of the rhubarb,
Lord of the roving cat, Lord of the cloud.
Blessed art Thou oh grapefruit King of the universe,
Blessed art Thou my sink, oh Blessed art Thou
Thou milkweed Queen of the sky, burster of seeds,
Who bringeth forth juice from the earth.

The Orange

CAMPBELL MCGRATH

Gone to swim after walking the boys to school.
Overcast morning, midweek, off-season,
few souls to brave the warm, storm-tossed waves,
not wild but rough for this tranquil coast.

Swimming now. In rhythm, arm over arm,
let the ocean buoy the body and the legs work little,
wave overhead, crash and roll with it, breathe,
stretch and build, windmill, climb the foam. Breathe,

breathe. Traveling downwind I make good time
and spot the marker by which I know to halt
and forge my way ashore. Who am I
to question the current? Surely this is peace abiding.

Walking back along the beach I mark the signs of erosion,
bide the usual flotsam of seagrass and fan coral,
a float from somebody's fishing boat,
crusted with sponge and barnacles, and then I find

the orange. Single irradiant sphere on the sand,
tide-washed, glistening as if new born,
golden orb, miraculous ur-fruit,
in all that sweep of horizon the only point of color.

Cross-legged on my towel I let the juice course
and mingle with the film of salt on my lips
and the sand in my beard as I steadily peel and eat it.
Considering the ancient lineage of this fruit,

the long history of its dispersal around the globe
on currents of animal and human migration,
and in light of the importance of the citrus industry
to the state of Florida, I will not claim

it was the best and sweetest orange in the world,
though it was, o great salt water
of eternity,
o strange and bountiful orchard.

The Tropics in New York

CLAUDE MCKAY

Bananas ripe and green, and ginger-root,
  Cocoa in pods and alligator pears,
And tangerines and mangoes and grape fruit,
  Fit for the highest prize at parish fairs,

Set in the window, bringing memories
  Of fruit-trees laden by low-singing rills,
And dewy dawns, and mystical blue skies
  In benediction over nun-like hills.

My eyes grew dim, and I could no more gaze;
  A wave of longing through my body swept,
And, hungry for the old, familiar ways,
  I turned aside and bowed my head and wept.

Pear Tree

H.D.

Silver dust,
lifted from the earth,
higher than my arms reach,
you have mounted,
O, silver,
higher than my arms reach,
you front us with great mass;

no flower ever opened
so staunch a white leaf,
no flower ever parted silver
from such rare silver;

O, white pear,
your flower-tufts
thick on the branch
bring summer and ripe fruits
in their purple hearts.

Sonnet

TERRANCE HAYES

We sliced the watermelon into smiles.
We sliced the watermelon into smiles.
We sliced the watermelon into smiles.
We sliced the watermelon into smiles.
We sliced the watermelon into smiles.
We sliced the watermelon into smiles.
We sliced the watermelon into smiles.
We sliced the watermelon into smiles.
We sliced the watermelon into smiles.
We sliced the watermelon into smiles.
We sliced the watermelon into smiles.
We sliced the watermelon into smiles.
We sliced the watermelon into smiles.
We sliced the watermelon into smiles.

Watermelons

CHARLES SIMIC

Green Buddhas
On the fruit stand.
We eat the smile
And spit out the teeth.

Strawberrying

MAY SWENSON

My hands are murder-red. Many a plump head
drops on the heap in the basket. Or, ripe
to bursting, they might be hearts, matching
the blackbird's wing-fleck. Gripped to a reed
he shrieks his ko-ka-ree in the next juicy field.
He's left his peck in some juicy cheeks, when
at first blush and mostly white, they showed
streaks of sweetness to the marauder.

We're picking near the shore, the morning
sunny, a slight wind moving rough-veined leaves
our hands rumple among. Fingers find by feel
the ready fruit in clusters. Flesh was perfect
yesterday. . . . June was for gorging. . . .
sweet hearts young and firm before decay.

"Take only the biggest, and not too ripe,"
a mother calls to her girl and boy, barefoot
in the furrows. "Don't step on any. Don't
change rows. Don't eat too many." Mesmerized
by the largesse, the children squat and pull
and pick handfulls of rich scarlets, half
for the baskets, half for avid mouths.
Soon, whole faces are stained.

A crop this thick begs for plunder. Ripeness
wants to be ravished, as udders of cows when hard,

the blue-veined bags distended, ache to be stripped.
Hunkered in mud between the rows, sun burning
the back of our necks, we grope for, and rip loose
soft nippled heads. If they bleed—too soft—
let them stay. Let them rot in the heat.

When, hidden away in a damp hollow under moldy
leaves, I come upon a clump of heart-shapes
once red, now spiderspit-gray, intact but empty,
still attached to their dead stems—
families smothered as at Pompeii—I rise
and stretch. I eat one more big ripe lopped
head. Red-handed, I leave the field.

Planting Strawberries

GERALD STERN

If this is a thing of the past,
planting strawberries on the Delaware River
and eating zucchini from my own garden,
then I will have to be buried too,
along with the beer-hall musicians
and the "startlingly beautiful sunset"
and the giant Swiss pansies,
in the ruins of Pennsylvania.
I put the strawberries in one by one.
They look like octopuses and their feet dance in the water
as I cover them up to their necks.
They take up so much room
that I could eat an acre of them for breakfast
sitting in the dirt.
What I like best is having a garden this close to
the factories and stores of Easton.
It is like carrying a knife in my pocket!
It is like kissing in the streets!
I would like to convert all the new spaces
back into trees and rocks.
I would like to turn the earth up after the bulldozers
have gone and plant corn and tomatoes.
I would like to guard our new property—with helmets and dogs.
I would like us to feed ourselves in the middle of their civilization.

Blackberries Are Back

WILLIAM STAFFORD

Blackberries are back. They cling near
little streams. Their eyes, bright mornings,
make tunnels through the vines.
They see their own thorns in the sky,
and the print of leaves.

At night they hide inside the wind,
ready to try the outdoors on.
They swing for distance, root for
fidelity. The truth is your only ransom
once they touch your tongue.

Blackberrying

SYLVIA PLATH

Nobody in the lane, and nothing, nothing but blackberries,
Blackberries on either side, though on the right mainly,
A blackberry alley, going down in hooks, and a sea
Somewhere at the end of it, heaving. Blackberries
Big as the ball of my thumb, and dumb as eyes
Ebon in the hedges, fat
With blue-red juices. These they squander on my fingers.
I had not asked for such a blood sisterhood; they must love me.
They accommodate themselves to my milkbottle, flattening their
 sides.

Overhead go the choughs in black, cacophonous flocks—
Bits of burnt paper wheeling in a blown sky.
Theirs is the only voice, protesting, protesting.
I do not think the sea will appear at all.
The high, green meadows are glowing, as if lit from within.
I come to one bush of berries so ripe it is a bush of flies,
Hanging their bluegreen bellies and their wing panes in a Chinese
 screen.
The honey-feast of the berries has stunned them; they believe in
 heaven.
One more hook, and the berries and bushes end.

The only thing to come now is the sea.
From between two hills a sudden wind funnels at me,
gapping its phantom laundry in my face.
These hills are too green and sweet to have tasted salt.

I follow the sheet path between them. A last hook brings me
To the hills' northern face, and the face is orange rock
That looks out on nothing, nothing but a great space
Of white and pewter lights, and a din like silversmiths
Beating and beating at an intractable metal.

Blackberries for Amelia

RICHARD WILBUR

Fringing the woods, the stone walls, and the lanes,
Old thickets everywhere have come alive,
Their new leaves reaching out in fans of five
From tangles overarched by this year's canes.

They have their flowers too, it being June,
And here or there in brambled dark-and-light
Are small, five-petaled blooms of chalky white,
As random-clustered and as loosely strewn

As the far stars, of which we now are told
That ever faster do they bolt away,
And that a night may come in which, some say,
We shall have only blackness to behold.

I have no time for any change so great,
But I shall see the August weather spur
Berries to ripen where the flowers were—
Dark berries, savage-sweet and worth the wait—

And there will come the moment to be quick
And save some from the birds, and I shall need
Two pails, old clothes in which to stain and bleed,
And a grandchild to talk with while we pick.

A Meeting

WENDELL BERRY

In a dream I meet
my dead friend. He has,
I know, gone long and far,
and yet he is the same
for the dead are changeless.
They grow no older.
It is I who have changed,
grown strange to what I was.
Yet I, the changed one,
ask: "How you been?"
He grins and looks at me.
"I been eating peaches
off some mighty fine trees."

The Weight of Sweetness

LI-YOUNG LEE

No easy thing to bear, the weight of sweetness.

Song, wisdom, sadness, joy: sweetness
equals three of any of these gravities.

See a peach bend
the branch and strain the stem until
it snaps.
Hold the peach, try the weight, sweetness
and death so round and snug
in your palm.
And, so, there is
the weight of memory:

Windblown, a rain-soaked
bough shakes, showering
the man and the boy.
They shiver in delight,
and the father lifts from his son's cheek
one green leaf
fallen like a kiss.

The good boy hugs a bag of peaches
his father has entrusted
to him.
Now he follows
his father, who carries a bagful in each arm.

See the look on the boy's face
as his father moves
faster and farther ahead, while his own steps
flag, and his arms grow weak, as he labors
under the weight
of peaches.

From Blossoms

LI-YOUNG LEE

From blossoms comes
this brown paper bag of peaches
we bought from the boy
at the bend in the road where we turned toward
signs painted *Peaches*.

From laden boughs, from hands,
from sweet fellowship in the bins,
comes nectar at the roadside, succulent
peaches we devour, dusty skin and all,
comes this familiar dust of summer, dust we eat.

O, to take what we love inside,
to carry within us an orchard, to eat
not only the skin, but the shade,
not only the sugar, but the days, to hold
the fruit in our hands, adore it, then bite into
the round jubilance of peach.

There are days we live
as if death were nowhere
in the background; from joy
to joy to joy, from wing to wing,
from blossom to blossom to
impossible blossom, to sweet impossible blossom.

PERMISSIONS

ACKNOWLEDGMENTS

Thanks first to Rob McQuilkin and Kathy Belden, my agent and editor, for their precision and support and last-minute suggestions. They always made working on this book enjoyable, and have only made the book better, as has the entire team at Bloomsbury USA. Thanks, too, to Rosemary Magee, who suggested the seed of this book years ago. Thanks to both my parents, both great yet very different cooks—I'm still learning what they tried to teach me, not just in the kitchen. Thanks, too, to my family at the Southern Foodways Alliance, the best organization I have ever worked with or for (not to mention providers of some of the best food I've ever eaten). Last but not least, thanks to Kate Tuttle, and not just for her help finding the title of this book; she sustains our whole family with meals and much more.

INDEX

A NOTE ON THE EDITOR

KEVIN YOUNG is the author of seven books of poetry, most recently *Ardency* and *Dear Darkness*. His collection *For the Confederate Dead* won the Paterson Poetry Prize for Sustained Literary Achievement, and *Jelly Roll* was a finalist for the National Book Award and the Los Angeles Times Book Prize. He is also the author of the nonfiction book *The Grey Album: On the Blackness of Blackness* and the editor of seven previous collections, including *The Best American Poetry 2011*; *The Art of Losing: Poems of Grief and Healing*; and *Blues Poems* and *Jazz Poems*, from the Everyman's Library Pocket Poets series. Young is currently the Atticus Haygood Professor of English and Creative Writing and curator of Literary Collections and the Raymond Danowski Poetry Library at Emory University in Atlanta.